How to Be a
People Helper
REVISED EDITION

How to Be a
PEOPLE
HELPER

GARY R. COLLINS

Tyndale House Publishers, Inc.
WHEATON, ILLINOIS

Library of Congress Cataloging-in-Publication Data

Collins, Gary R.
  How to be a people helper / Gary R. Collins. —Rev. ed.
    p.   cm.
  Includes bibliographical references and index.
  ISBN 0-8423-1385-0
  1. Helping behavior. 2. Counseling. 3. Pastoral counseling.
4. Peer counseling in the church. I. Title.
BF637.H4C64 1995   94-34388
253—dc20

CONTENTS

"If it ain't broke, don't fix it!"

I don't know where I first heard this piece of wisdom, but it has come to mind several times as I have worked on this book revision.

Almost twenty years ago, following a series of lectures in Colorado, some people in the audience suggested that my talks should be revised and put into a book. A couple of years passed before I took the time to do this, and after finishing the manuscript, I put it into a file drawer and got busy with other things. Some time later I mentioned it in passing to a publisher friend who convinced me to dust it off so he could bring it into print. The resulting book was well received, sold more copies than any other book that I have written, and eventually was translated into several foreign languages. For more than fifteen years it has continued to be available.

The principles that were part of that first book are still relevant—so "if it ain't broke, why fix it?"

The answer is that many changes have occurred since this book originally appeared—changes in counseling techniques, approaches to training, research findings, and types of problems. Most dramatic, perhaps, have been changes in attitudes toward counseling.

In the original book, for example, I wrote these words in the second paragraph:

> Until now, little has been written to assist the Christian lay counselor (or *paraprofessional*, to use the term by which these

people are usually described in the psychological literature).
Almost nothing exists in print to show that counseling can
and must be a vital part of the church's outreach to others.
Several years ago we came to realize that evangelism was not
a responsibility only for pastors and Billy Graham. Books
began to be written which showed that evangelism was the
task of laymen who were trained by church leaders. Now the
time has come for us to make the same shift in the area of
counseling. The layman, especially the Christian layman,
must take greater responsibility in meeting the needs of those
who seek solace, friendship, or counsel. People helping is not
something that we can leave solely to professionals or busy
pastors.

Since these words were written, there has been a groundswell
of interest in lay counseling. During the past couple of decades,
a variety of books and training programs have appeared in both
secular and Christian communities. Lay counseling is now
well accepted. Thus, one of the original purposes for this book
is gone; there is no longer a need to convince believers that we
should be people helpers. Most are already convinced.

Despite the competing books, however, this little volume
has continued to be the basis of people-helper training
programs in a number of churches, colleges, and Christian
organizations. In the original book, I sought to give practical
guidelines for helping others—guidelines that were clear, easy
to grasp, free of complicated psychological jargon, biblically
based, concise, and psychologically accurate. I have the same
goal for this second edition.

In many respects, therefore, the first edition "ain't broke,"
but it *is* outdated. For this reason it needs to be *fixed* and
brought into the nineties and early twenty-first century. New
information and more recent research findings have been
incorporated into the following pages along with some fresh

conclusions about helping. This new edition adds information on stress, gives more detailed people-helping techniques, points to some of the recent books and articles on lay counseling, avoids the sexist language that appeared earlier, and adds a few examples. Once again, I have written about methods without trying to summarize information concerning specific problems, such as depression, anxiety, marital conflict, or habit disorders. Other books give information about these and similar topic areas.[1]

Originally, *How to Be a People Helper* was part of a training program designed to teach people-helping skills to laypersons. Several years ago the training manual that accompanied this book was taken out of print, but I have continued to get letters from people who are still trying to find copies of that old workbook. In place of a new and updated workbook, the end of this book includes learning exercises for each of the following chapters. This allows you to read this book in one of three ways. You can read the text and skip the rest. You can read the text and try to do the exercises yourself. Or you can read the text and then meet with a group of others to do the exercises together and to practice what you have learned. This third approach will do the most to help you become a better people helper. To assist in this, a videotape package is available to guide individual or group study.

We should not assume that we learn to be effective people helpers solely by reading a book, any more than you can learn to play the piano or to swim by reading a book. People helping involves interaction with others. The best people helpers are those who practice their helping skills and who are involved in the lives of others.

As you read the following pages, you will notice that the word *counseling* is not used very much. Counseling is a good word, and much of what lay people do is counseling. But I prefer to reserve the word *counseling* for those people who have training in the helping professions and who focus attention on helping others with personal problems. *People helping* suggests something broader. People helpers do talk face-to-face with others about their problems, but people helping goes beyond this and is more consistent with terms like *caregiving, encouragement, meeting needs, reaching out, giving support,* or *friend-to-friend helping.* Many of us will never be counselors; all of us are called to be people helpers.

This revised edition, like the one that came before, is based on the belief that people helping (and Christian counseling) must be built on the Bible, God's Word, and must be consistent with the Great Commission, in which Jesus commanded his followers to make disciples of all nations. So relevant is the concept of discipleship that we discuss this in the first chapter.

From this it does not follow that competent people helpers will disregard the techniques of psychology, psychiatry, or the other helping professions. There is no attempt to discredit the counseling profession or to suggest that highly trained counselors are unnecessary. I number myself among those who are called professional counselors, and I respect many of my colleagues. But I also recognize (as do many of my professional colleagues) that many people can be effective people helpers even though they have little or no training. This book is written to help them—to help you—to be better people helpers; to do this caring work with greater skill and efficiency.

Many people, especially my wife, Julie, have been people helpers to me as I have worked on this book. In addition, I deeply appreciate the continuing friendship of Lawrence Tornquist, who made a significant contribution to the first edition of the book; to my daughter Lynn Collins, who typed portions of the following pages (thus saving some of my time at the word processor); and to Timothy Clinton and Ron Beers, who encouraged me to do this revision. Joy Olson, my administrative assistant, has psychological expertise and people skills that have protected me from interruptions and contributed in many ways to the completion of this project. Special thanks go to Brett Helvie, who helped with the research for this book, wrote most of the study questions, worked with me in the production of the training program, gave his insights into the rewritten manuscript, and prepared the index.

Over the years, I have presented many of the following concepts to many audiences both in North America and overseas. I am grateful for the responses that have come from these people, from students, from helpees, and from others who have written to me about people helping. Many of these unnamed people have helped to refine my earlier ideas and have made this a better book than the one that came before. Maybe that first edition did, indeed, need some fixing!

I hope that the following pages will be interesting and useful. Most of all, I pray that this book will help you to become a more skilled Christian people helper who serves Christ by helping others.

Gary R. Collins

Notes
1. See, for example, my book *Christian Counseling: A Comprehensive Guide,* rev. ed. (Dallas: Word, 1988).

CHAPTER ONE

The Heart of
People Helping

WOULD *anybody ever stop?*
John and Tib Sherrill must have wondered, standing in the blazing August sun, next to their disabled car. Highway I-75 is a busy road, especially in the summer when thousands of vacationing families head for the tourist attractions of Florida. For an hour and a half cars sped by while the Sherrills watched. Nobody even slowed. Maybe the passing motorists were in too much of a hurry to even notice the stranded couple. Perhaps they were afraid to get involved with strangers. Others may have rushed by, assuming that somebody else would stop.

Eventually somebody did. An old mud-splattered pickup pulled over to the side of the road and backed up to the stalled car. The driver was a young farmer clad in overalls caked with gray mud. Emerging from his vehicle, he uttered only one word.

"Problemas?"

The man spoke almost no English, but he looked under the car hood, shook his head, and waved the Sherrills into his pickup.

Together they rode for twenty miles to the next exit, where the farmer took his passengers to the nearest garage, waited to be sure that they would get help, and headed back to his truck. John reached for his wallet to pay the man for his trouble, but the farmer smiled and shook his head. They all exchanged handshakes, and the man was gone.

Soon the car was repaired, and the couple continued on their way, filled with thanks for the Good Samaritan who had stopped after so many others had passed by. Surely they would never see him again. There was no way to repay him for his kindness, but John had another idea. He determined to stop and offer help to the next stranded driver that he saw along the way. Better still, he said to his wife, "Let's stop and help the next ten."

"Forming that high-minded resolve was one thing; acting on it was another," John wrote in an article telling about his experiences. He knew that stopping could be dangerous, and he had to be careful. But he asked God to guide.

The first opportunity came several months later when the Sherrills saw a family stopped beside the road in New Jersey. The man had run out of gas, so the couple drove him to the nearest filling station.

That night, when they were unpacking their car, they found the man's wallet where it had fallen on the floor of the backseat.

"I hope you weren't worried," John said when he called to say that the wallet would be mailed the next morning.

"Of course not," the man replied. "Would the Good Samaritan steal?"

Over three years have passed since the Spanish-speaking

farmer stopped to help the Sherrills in Florida. Since that time they have stopped many times to offer help—more than the promised ten. In each case, they have refused payment and instead have told the story of their own experiences. The reactions have often been similar: "I'm going to do the same thing! I'm going to help people like you are doing."

John and Tib Sherrill are people helpers. Maybe they have never had a course in counseling, but they have helped a lot of stranded individuals in times of need.[1]

You Can Be a People Helper

People helping is everybody's business. Psychologists, psychiatrists, social workers, pastors, and other professionals have special expertise in this area, but in one way or another all of us have opportunities to be people helpers almost every day. Guiding our children through a crisis, comforting a bereaved neighbor in a time of grief, advising a teenager about a dating problem, listening to a relative describe the problems with a wayward son or daughter, encouraging the family of an alcoholic, helping one's mate cope with a difficult work situation, guiding a young Christian through a period of doubt—all of these are helping situations. And so is helping a stranded motorist at the side of the road.

Despite the many professionals in our stress-filled culture, most problems are handled by lay people, whether or not they feel qualified. Even if there could be a sufficient number of professional and pastoral counselors to handle everybody's needs, some people still would prefer to discuss their problems with a relative, neighbor, or friend. Friends are close by, they don't charge fees, they are available, and often they are easier to talk to than a stranger who goes by some awesome title like "psychiatrist," "therapist," or "counselor." Nonprofessional people helpers may have little or no training, but they make a significant impact nevertheless. These people—individuals like the Sherrills or like you—are on the front lines of the battle against stress, confusion, and mental illness.

People Helping and the Great Commission

Shortly before he left this earth to go back to heaven, Jesus gave his famous mandate to the little band of followers who had gathered with him on the mountain in Galilee. "Go and make disciples of all nations," he said, "baptizing them in the name of the Father and of the Son and of the Holy Spirit, and teaching them to obey everything I have commanded you." Jesus assured the disciples of his complete authority and presence with them "always, to the very end of the age" (Matt. 28:19-20).

Then he left.

The men and women to whom Jesus spoke were already disciples. They had made the decision to follow Jesus and to commit their lives fully to him. They must have understood, at least partially, that because of divine love, Christ had come into the world to die in the place of sinful human beings. They must have admitted and confessed their sin and submitted completely to the risen Lord. This was the dedicated group to whom Jesus gave a twofold responsibility. Discipling was to involve *telling* people about Jesus, with the goal of bringing them to the point where they would decide to become Christ's followers, and *teaching* others what Jesus himself had taught during his brief time on earth.

Jesus taught that all of us are created in the image of God and loved by him. But we also are sinners in need of a savior. Jesus attacked the idea that a person is a child of God because of citizenship, parental beliefs, religious affiliation, or good works. Instead, Jesus proclaimed that if any person wants to

have eternal life in heaven and abundant life on earth, he or
she must abandon human schemes to reach God or to earn
his favor. Instead, it is necessary to confess sin and to yield
one's whole life to Christ's control. The death of Jesus was
to pay the penalty for human sin and to make it possible,
for those who wanted to do so, to become children of God
(John 3:16; 10:10; Rom. 3:23; 5:8; 10:9). The disciples were
instructed to proclaim this message, to urge people to put
their faith in Christ, to baptize the new believers, and to
teach them from the Scriptures.

Somebody has suggested that the Lord began his ministry
by calling a little group of twelve to *become* disciples, that
he ended his ministry with the Great Commission to *make*
disciples, and that in between he taught people how to
be disciples. In this process, Jesus approached people in a
variety of ways. At different times he instructed, listened,
preached, argued, encouraged, condemned, and demonstrated what it was like to be a true child of God. Perhaps
no two persons were ever approached in exactly the same
way. Jesus recognized individual differences in personality,
need, and level of understanding. And he treated people
accordingly.

The Scope of the Great Commission

It does not appear that the Great Commission was
limited to one geographical area or to one period of history.
Neither is there any indication that the instructions of
Jesus were limited to a few people, such as pastors or other
church leaders. Instead, it was Jesus' intent that all of his
followers, for generations to come, would be in the business
of making disciples—involved in outreach to nonbelievers
and in teaching new believers.

The Great Commission has relevance for Christians today.

Since being a disciple and making disciples are requirements
for all Christians, surely the discipling of others must be a
part of Christian counseling and people helping—perhaps
even the major goal.

The Meaning of Discipleship

Before pursuing this controversial suggestion, it is important to think about the meaning of discipleship. In its broad-
est sense the word *disciple* means "student" or "learner." As
used in the Scriptures, however, the term has a much stronger
connotation. It implies the acceptance of views and teachings
from a leader to whom we are obedient. A disciple wants to
learn from his master and become like that person in charac-
ter (Luke 6:40).

The people who enroll in my classes are my students, but
they are not my disciples. They learn from me, but they do
not follow me in obedience and dedication. Their goal is not
to become like me. In contrast, Jesus came into the world to
make disciples who would learn from him, obey him, become
like him, and follow him. He spent his life discipling men
and women. Then, at the end of his earthly life he commanded each of us to follow his example by making disciples
of Christ. By implication he gave us the task of making disciplers who could carry on the task.

The Characteristics of Discipleship

According to the Scriptures a disciple has at least three
characteristics, is called upon to pay three costs, and is given
three responsibilities. As we will see, all of this is important
for people who call themselves Christians; all can be of crucial
significance to those who want to be Christian people helpers.

We will look first at the three characteristics of a disciple of
Jesus Christ: obedience, love, and fruitfulness.

Obedience

A disciple is a person who is committed to and obedient to the person and teachings of the master. It is possible to be a curious onlooker who makes observations about Jesus, a student who learns from Jesus, or a scholar who carefully analyzes the teachings of Jesus, but these people are not disciples. The disciple hears the words "Come, follow me" (Matt. 4:19) and decides to do so with complete submission and willingness to obey.

To be obedient to Jesus Christ is to place oneself under the authority of God and of the living Word of God (John 1:1, 14). According to Jesus, we are truly his disciples when we hold to his words and teachings (John 8:31; 15:7). This would imply letting the Word of God exert absolute control over our life. It involves obediently seeking to bring every aspect of life into conformity with biblical teaching.

Love

The second characteristic of a disciple is love. In John 13:34-35, Jesus gave his disciples a "new command" to love one another (see also John 15:12, 17). "As I have loved you, so you must love one another. By this all men will know that you are my disciples, if you love one another." Love has been called the mark of the Christian. Of course, we all fail to live up to this standard, and churches sometimes are characterized more by conflict than by compassion. Nevertheless, love is to be the most obvious and unique characteristic of the disciple of Jesus Christ. It is the most basic requirement for any person who would seek to be a people helper.

When the apostle John was writing his first epistle, he realized that some of his readers were having difficulty knowing who were really Christians and who were not. To help with this problem John indicated that real Christians are people characterized by love. If a person doesn't have love, John said, he or she probably isn't even a believer (1 John 4:7-11). It is a contradiction of terms to think that one could be a true follower of Christ and not be loving.

Fruitfulness

It is "to my Father's glory," Jesus stated, "that you bear much fruit, showing yourselves to be my disciples" (John 15:8). Fruitfulness is the third characteristic of a disciple.

We live in a society where almost everybody wants to be successful and where many of us have personal plans for reaching this goal. Some well-meaning Christians have dreams about successful ministries, and they are working diligently to make their dreams come true. In John 15, however, Jesus told his followers that all of these efforts would be useless unless individual disciples were committed to Christ, abiding in him, and not trying to push ahead with their own schemes, dependent on their own resources. Jesus used the example of grapevines that were not producing fruit. The best thing for them, he said, was that they should be broken off from the vine and burned in a fire.

It is sobering to realize that God might come along someday and destroy our self-centered work (2 Pet. 3:10). But some things will never be destroyed, including God's Word (Isa. 40:8) and God's people (John 5:28-29). In setting life objectives, therefore, disciples give themselves to understanding the Word of God and building the people who have been created by God.

On the night of his betrayal, Jesus gathered the disciples into the upper room and spent one last teaching session with them. His words are recorded in John 13–17. After the evening meal was served, Jesus took a basin of water and

washed the disciples' feet. This was a supreme act of humil-
ity and servanthood. "You call me 'Teacher' and 'Lord,' and
rightly so, for that is what I am," Jesus said when he
rejoined the disciples at the table. Then he added that they
should follow his example and be servants. "I have set you
an example that you should do as I have done for you." To
be really fruitful, true disciples need to be like their Master.
They must be servants (John 13:13-15).

The Costs of Discipleship

The Bible never promises that it will be easy to follow
Christ and to be a disciple. True servants must be willing
to surrender time, energy, personal comfort, and sometimes
money in an effort to please the Master and help others.
Because there are costs to being a disciple, nobody can be
recruited by arm twisting or manipulation. Becoming a
disciple is a voluntary commitment, kept only by those
who realize the demands and are willing to pay the cost.
Of course, strong benefits come to the follower of Christ.
When we are weary or anxious, for example, we can freely
cast our cares on Jesus, who is compassionate and willing to
carry our burdens (Matt. 11:28-30; 1 Pet. 5:7). But to be a
disciple of Jesus Christ also means that we must be willing
to give up our closest relationships, our cherished ambitions, and our personal possessions (Luke 14:33).

Personal relationships
Consider first our personal relationships. Jesus never tore
down the family. On the contrary, he instructed us to respect
our parents, teach our children without exasperating them,
and love our mates. Nevertheless, the relationship that we
have with Christ must take precedence even over the family
(Luke 14:25-26).

Apparently, some Christian workers interpret this to mean that they can go about "the Lord's work" and leave their families to fend on their own. Such behavior forgets that raising a family and fulfilling our obligations as family members *is* the Lord's work as much as pastoring a church, teaching the Bible, or serving as a deacon. Surely God will hold us responsible for what we have done with the people in our families, but in terms of priorities, we must be willing to put Christ first in our lives, even before our family members.

Personal ambitions

For many career-centered people, it may be even harder to lay aside our personal ambitions. In Luke 9, after five thousand people had been fed, the disciples must have felt like they were part of something big and very successful. At that point, Jesus announced that discipleship involves denying oneself (including one's personal ambitions), taking up a cross (symbol of low status and death), and following Christ (Luke 9:23-25). Sometimes, of course, God does permit the disciple to attain a high status and often he or she is able to reach personal and financial goals. But the disciple must be willing to abandon personal ambitions or to have ambitions changed so that they conform to what Christ wants for our lives.

The cost of commitment does not seem to be emphasized much as we move into a new century; Charles Colson has called commitment "a lost value in American life." [2] Perhaps there are many of us who fear that commitment will lead to a life of misery and drudgery. Gone will be our plans to become successful career builders, and instead God might send us to be missionaries in some snake-infested jungle or crime-infested inner city. The implication is that commitment to Christ leads to second best.

But surely God never gives second best to his followers—even though from our limited perspectives we may think this is what we have received. God always gives what is best for us when we yield our personal ambitions to him. Few are willing to take this risk.

Personal possessions

Discipleship may also cost us our possessions. Riches, health, fame, material goods—none of these is wrong in itself, and often God gives these things in abundance. But they become wrong when they are made the chief ends of life.

Several years ago my wife and I were in the market for another house. We had outgrown our old house and felt the need for more space. One evening we made a list of everything we wanted: fireplace, dishwasher, separate dining room, air-conditioning, full basement, deck or patio, two-car attached garage, place for an office, good location, nice view—and more. Before long we began to ask why we wanted all of these things—including some that we couldn't really afford. Were we being pulled into the standards of a culture that measures success by the size of one's house or the make and model of one's car? Were we being caught in a way of thinking that measures personal worth by the abundance of our possessions?

Our house hunting reminded us that in eternity a person's value will not be measured by what he or she possessed on earth. All of our possessions, including money, homes, automobiles, labor-saving gadgets, stereo equipment, and other toys, come from the hand of God. All belong to God, must be surrendered to God, and should be used in ways that ultimately enable us to be better disciples of Jesus Christ and disciplers of others. "Any of you who does not give up everything he has cannot be my disciple," Jesus told his followers (Luke

11

14:33). A striving for personal possessions and adherence to an affluent lifestyle will squelch our effectiveness in obeying Christ's Great Commission.

The Responsibilities of Discipleship

In addition to the costs, being a disciple involves at least three responsibilities.

Outreach

Many years ago I first read about the little island of Iona, off the coast of Scotland. It was there that early Christians withdrew from the "world" so they could study, pray, find inspiration, worship, and plan strategy before leaving the island and scattering throughout Scotland with the gospel. When they were tired and in need of refreshment, they returned to Iona to rest and recuperate before scattering again.[3]

The island was a place of prayer and strengthening, as little like the world as possible. Some have suggested that the church should be like this: a place for refreshment and preparation of saints who are committed to evangelistic outreach. In practice it doesn't always work that way. Believers come to the church, where they are surrounded by other believers, who send out the gospel message through a foreign missionary or over the air waves from the comfort of air-conditioned television studios. In our efforts to be relevant, we try to be as much like the world as possible, and we expect nonbelievers to come to us. There is little serious Bible study or preparation for evangelism. As a result, we aren't very effective as witnesses, and we don't grow much as disciples.

The true disciple is responsible to witness for Christ. This does not mean withdrawing from all nonbelievers; it means that by following Paul's example we must search for common ground with non-Christians, hoping ultimately that some will be led to Christ (1 Cor. 9:19-22).

According to one writer,[4] this outreach, or evangelism, includes three factors: (1) proclamation of the gospel so that men and women might understand their sinfulness, God's offer of saving grace, and the need for their response to obtain salvation; (2) bringing people to a decision of faith in Christ and a commitment of their lives to him, resulting in their justification by God and their new birth into his spiritual family; and (3) public declaration of this new allegiance to Jesus Christ.

Bringing others to maturity

A second responsibility of the disciple is to bring others to maturity. God uses committed believers to accomplish this task and appears to work in a variety of ways. Sometimes, for example, older believers serve as examples or models of what mature Christianity should be like (1 Thess. 2:8; 1 Tim. 4:12). New believers are taught and given information (2 Tim. 3:15-17), confronted with the difficulties of discipleship (Luke 14:25-33), and given practical experience in serving (Mark 6:7).

Most often, this maturation process is not dependent on only one human teacher. It comes as new believers and those who are more advanced in the faith meet together on a regular basis. As a community of believers, they worship together, hear teaching from the Word of God, spur one another to love and good deeds, and grow into a loving, caring, mutually accountable body of Christians (Eph. 4:16; Heb. 10:24-25). In these ways, disciples learn from one another and build up each other. Maturity comes because each one spends time with God privately, learns from mentors and models who are more mature spiritually (1 Cor. 11:1), and meets regularly with a supportive group of fellow Christians.

Making Disciplers

The disciple also has the responsibility of making disciplers—training those who can go forth to disciple others. Paul outlined this explicitly when he wrote to Timothy: "Be strong in the grace that is in Christ Jesus. And the things you have heard me say in the presence of many witnesses entrust to reliable men who will also be qualified to teach others" (2 Tim. 2:1-2). Discipleship is a multiplication process in which those who are disciples disciple others, who in turn become disciplers. God never intended Christians to accept the gospel and then do nothing further. He intended that we should become his disciples, with all of the characteristics, costs, and responsibilities that this involves, and then go forth to make additional disciples for Christ.

Discipleship and People Helping

The emphasis on discipleship is so central to the teachings of the New Testament and so basic to the Christian way of life that it cannot be ignored when the Christian enters a counseling or other helping relationship. Of course, the people helper is not a manipulator, committed to pushing religion onto unsuspecting people who want to talk about personal problems. In counseling, as in most other relationships, it is not usual to raise religious issues immediately. But the Great Commission, servanthood, and discipleship are at the core of the Christian message, so they must be a prime concern in the mind of the believer who is involved in helping relationships.

The people helper who takes the Great Commission seriously will be different from the non-Christian helper. All good counselors periodically look inward at their own lives, seeking to be aware of their own psychological hang-ups and attempting to change (perhaps with the help of another counselor). But the Christian people helper also must be involved in a spiritual self-examination. "Am I really committed to Christ?" the helper must ask. "Am I teachable—since no Christian is right all the time? Do I discipline myself to grow spiritually? Am I faithfully involved in a local body of believers? Am I sensitive to the Holy Spirit's leading, seeking to purge the sin from my life, growing as a disciple of Jesus Christ, and sincerely interested in the spiritual growth of others?"

It is possible to answer no to each of these questions and to still help people. Successful secular therapists demonstrate this every day and so do many caring Christians. None of us has "arrived" spiritually, and even the most committed believers are still growing. But people helping that leaves out the spiritual dimension ultimately has something missing. It may stimulate good feelings and help people to cope with stress, but it does nothing to prepare people for eternity or to help them experience the abundant life here on earth—an abundance that comes only with commitment to Christ (John 10:10).

The disciple of Jesus Christ hopes that in time his or her helpees (people who receive help whom others may refer to as "counselees," "clients," or "patients") will consider the teachings of Christ, commit their lives to him, and grow in their knowledge of Jesus Christ. This is not to imply that evangelism and spiritual maturing are the only—or even the major—goals in counseling, but they are crucially important goals that even Christian people helpers are inclined to ignore or overlook.

Three Approaches to People Helping

Within the past several decades, the volume of information and research findings about counseling has exploded. Even with the help of computers few of us can keep up-to-date, and it no longer is possible for any one person to be aware of all developments in the field. There are literally thousands of counseling techniques and hundreds of approaches to people helping. For our purposes, however, we will mention three major approaches, each of which is used by Christians.

Humanistic secular approaches

These approaches to helping people say nothing about God. The counselor uses methods that help others deal with problems, gain insights, change behavior, make decisions, or in other ways give help without any reference to Christian spiritual issues.

"God as helper" approaches

These approaches have goals similar to those of the secular therapists, but the counselor or other helper acknowledges, at least privately, that God is a source of guidance and wisdom, a divine helper who responds to our prayers and guides in the helping process. Spiritual issues are not avoided if they come up in conversation, and sometimes God is even mentioned in the counseling session. Often, however, the counselor never says anything about God, and the person who comes for help might never be aware that his or her counselor is a believer.

Theocentric approaches

Different from the other approaches are those that we might term *theocentric*. These approaches assume that an eternal God exists who has ultimate purposes for the human race. God is assumed to be present in the counseling relationship, using the helper as his instrument to bring changes in the helpee's life. Hopefully, these changes will restore harmony between the helpee and God, improve personal relationships with others, help to reduce inner conflicts, improve the ability to deal with stress, give strength to cope with suffering, and instill the personal "peace of God which transcends all understanding" (Phil. 4:7).

The disciple who is also a helper strives for this theocentric approach. Empowered by the Holy Spirit, he or she is willing to develop the characteristics, pay the costs, and bear the responsibilities of discipleship. In turn, the helper becomes God's instrument for bringing changes in the lives of those to whom help is given.

The Diversity of Christian Counseling

It is unrealistic to expect that we ever will arrive at one biblical approach to counseling and people helping, any more than we have discovered one biblical approach to missions, evangelism, Christian education, systematic theology, or preaching. To a large extent, helping techniques depend on the personality, training, talents, and theological beliefs of the helper, and on the nature of the helpee's problems. Instead of trying to find and push for one "true" Christian counseling theory or approach to helping, we should seek to uncover the various techniques and counseling approaches that arise out of or are clearly consistent with the teachings of Scripture. Then we should try these methods, not using subjective feelings as proof that we are "really helping people," but using carefully controlled evaluation and assessment techniques. Many of the established methods for helping will be mentioned in the pages that follow.

The place to begin a Christian approach to counseling, however, is with the Bible, and there can be no more basic starting point than the Great Commission given by Jesus himself. This is a blueprint for building the church, and it forms a foundation on which to build lives and interpersonal relationships through people helping.

Notes

1. John Sherrill, "My Samaritan Experiment," *Guideposts*, February 1990, 171–74.
2. Ted W. Engstrom, forward to *A Time for Commitment* (Grand Rapids: Zondervan, 1987). See also Jerry White, *The Power of Commitment* (Colorado Springs: NavPress, 1985); Edward Dayton, *What Ever Happened to Commitment?* (Grand Rapids: Zondervan, 1984); and Crawford W. Loritts, Jr., *A Passionate Commitment* (San Bernardino, Calif.: Here's Life Publishers, 1989).
3. This one-paragraph description is a simplistic summary of the early days of the community of believers, established on Iona in A.D. 563. In 1988, Collins Fount Books in Britain published a history of the Iona community, including events in the 1930s when the ruined abbey of Iona was rebuilt, and a new community was established. The book is written by Ron Ferguson and entitled *Chasing the Wild Goose: The Iona Community.*
4. Allan Coppedge, *The Biblical Principles of Discipleship* (Grand Rapids: Zondervan, 1989), 115.

The Basics of People Helping

WHAT IS a Christian people helper? Do the Christian and nonbeliever have different goals in helping others? If we take the Bible seriously, will this influence how we deal with other people? Can there be biblically based approaches to helping that allow for personality differences in the helpers, uniqueness in each helpee, and the diversity of problems that we encounter in helping situations? Can a Christian learn from and use counseling theories and techniques that secular therapists have developed and shown to be effective, or do we have to throw out all psychology—as some recent writers have proposed?

These kinds of questions concerned me many years ago after I received my degree in clinical psychology and went to work in a university counseling center. I had a diploma to prove that I was trained as a professional psychologist, but I didn't feel very competent in spite of all my education in several reputable graduate schools. As a Christian it seemed that

I ought to be doing something more than following the secular methods that I had been taught, but I didn't know how to do anything different or better. Employed in the counseling center of a state university, I couldn't talk much about religion and still keep my job, but I knew that the gospel of Jesus Christ had something to say to those lonely and frustrated kids who were coming every day to my office.

While I worked in that counseling center I think I helped a lot of people, and my employer appeared to be happy with my work. But I wasn't satisfied. After several months on the job, I decided that my abilities were better suited to teaching, so I left the counseling center and went to work in the psychology department of a midwestern liberal arts college. Teaching was a rewarding experience. I enjoyed the students and the study, but my insecurities about counseling persisted.

Then I met Paul Tournier.

Discipleship Counseling

Following Tournier's death a few years ago, his books faded in popularity, but until the early 1980s, this man was known worldwide and highly regarded as a Christian people helper. His writing style could be difficult to follow, and readers did not always agree with his theology or conclusions, but Paul Tournier must have helped thousands through his counseling, his speaking, and his books. He traveled often, especially in later life, and his writings were translated into numerous foreign languages.

Tournier lived in a suburb of Geneva, in the French-speaking part of Switzerland. For several months my family and I lived nearby so I could learn from Tournier and write a book about him.[1] He was a genuinely humble, compassionate, and godly man who took the Bible seriously, consistently demonstrated Christian love, tried to keep aware of trends in the counseling field, and recognized that every helper is in some ways unique. In meeting with him I began to see, for the first time, something of the potential of Christian counseling. Tournier didn't propose any formal system of counseling, but he nevertheless developed a basically biblical approach to helping people. And he taught me that counseling could work.

Many writers have proposed approaches that claim to be biblical and are assumed to be effective. Some Christians maintain that they have the "true biblical" approach to helping and that all others are wrong. This confuses a lot of people. How can we be Christians, they ask, and have such a variety of counseling systems, all of which claim to come from the Bible?

We need to remember that counselors, like theologians and Bible students, are fallible human beings. We see things from different perspectives. Committed Presbyterians disagree with committed Baptists on important issues—yet all may be Christian and determined to be biblical. As we have seen, there are different biblically based approaches to preaching (homiletics) or Bible interpretation (hermeneutics), even though each may seek to be faithful to the Word of God.

The same is true in counseling. Because of the differences, we can learn from each other, recognizing that human beings will never have the perfect theory of counseling until we get to heaven. Then counseling will no longer be needed!

As long as we remain on earth, however, if we are to take the Bible seriously in our counseling, we cannot ignore the Great Commission. Even though we may use different methods or learn from different teachers, Christian people helpers know that the command to go into the world and make disciples is a major tenet of New Testament teaching. So important, in fact, is the concept of discipleship in

Scripture that we might think of Christian counseling as *discipleship counseling.*[2]

Discipleship counseling (*servant counseling* might be an equally accurate term) is a broad and general approach to helping others that seeks to build on the teachings of the Bible. It is a view of helping that recognizes the centrality of the Great Commission and has the discipling of others as a core goal. It assumes that the God who speaks through the Bible has also revealed truth about his universe through science, including psychology. Thus, psychological methods and techniques are taken seriously, but they must be tested, not only scientifically and pragmatically, but primarily against the written Word of God.

The discipleship approach uses a variety of methods for helping others. These depend, in part, on the helpee's needs, personality, and problems. The goals of people helping also depend, in part, on the needs and desires of those who seek our help. In general, however, people helpers seek to assist individuals and families to:

- function more effectively in their daily lives;
- find freedom from spiritual, psychological, and interpersonal conflicts;
- be at peace with themselves and to enjoy a growing communion with God;
- develop and maintain smooth interpersonal relationships;
- learn and use effective skills for living; and
- be actively involved in becoming disciples of and disciplers for Jesus Christ.

We might think of Christian people helping as having three basic functions: a *prophetic* task that involves knowing and sharing the written Word of God as found in the Bible; a *liberating* task that seeks to free people from spiritual, personal, and interpersonal problems or conflicts; and an *empowering* task that attempts to teach, enable, and equip people to live more fulfilling, balanced, and Christ-honoring lives.

The discipleship approach can be expressed in terms of six people-helper principles. Four of these are presented in this chapter. The others are in chapter 3.

People-Helper Principle No. 1: The Helper

In any helping relationship, the personality, values, attitudes, and beliefs of the helper are of primary importance. In writing to the Christians in Galatia, Paul instructed the believers to "restore" (bring to a state of wholeness) any individual who was having personal difficulties (Gal. 6:1). Apparently some of the Galatians were lapsing into sin, and as a result, they were having problems. These men and women were of concern to the apostle, but notice who was to give them help: "you who are spiritual."

In chapter 5 of Galatians we read the well-known listing of those traits that characterize spiritual Christians: love, joy, peace, patience, kindness, goodness, faithfulness, gentleness, and self-control (Gal. 5:22-23). Spiritual individuals strive to bring their values into conformity with the teaching of Jesus, are led by the Spirit of God, and are not self-centered, conceited, troublemakers, or inclined to be envious (Gal. 5:25-26).

Instead, the Christian people helper is gentle, even with a person who has been caught in a sin (Gal. 6:1). Of course there are times when we need to be firm in talking to others, but even then we seek to be compassionate and respectful.

Christian people helpers are aware of the temptations that come to those who work with others intimately, and take care to prevent any of their own helping relationships from becoming sinful (Gal. 6:1). The caregiver is willing to help bear the burdens of others in a loving, compassionate manner, even when this might be painful and inconvenient (v. 2). Biblical helpers are humble (v. 3), recognizing that their strength and wisdom come from the Lord, so there is no place for a superior, holier-than-thou manner. Helpers, in addition, are self-examining—inclined to evaluate themselves realistically and to avoid comparisons with others (v. 4). Helpers are willing to both give and receive from others, and there is recognition that each person must bear responsibility for his or her behavior (vv. 5-8). The biblical helper is aware of God and of spiritual influences in human behavior (vv. 7-8), and he or she tries to be patient (v. 9) even when the helping task is long and arduous. The helper recognizes a responsibility to do good to all people, but "especially to those who belong to the family of believers" (v. 10).

To this long list, we might add that the best Christian helpers are interested in people, genuinely eager to help, inclined to show respect, able to keep confidences, and willing to learn. Helpers can be of any age, but the most effective are those who have had some personal experiences in dealing with the stresses of life. Good helpers also are psychologically stable and not trying to deal with their own problems by counseling others. (Unstable people almost never succeed as people helpers—at least until they are able to deal with their own insecurities.)

Does this leave you feeling overwhelmed? The standards for a good helper are high, but they are attainable. These standards should characterize all Christians who are walking in a close daily relationship with Jesus Christ. It does not follow, of course, that every committed believer is automatically a good people helper. Some basic skills are involved in effective helping, and these need to be learned. But the person who seeks to build a close relationship with Jesus Christ develops characteristics that might be summarized in one word: *love.* As we have seen, love is crucially important in people helping.

Many of these conclusions are consistent with psychological research that has shown how the personal traits of the helper may be as important to good counseling as the methods that are used.[3] Some evidence suggests that effective helpers succeed, not so much because of their theoretical orientation or techniques, but because of their empathy, warmth, and genuineness.

Empathy comes from a German word that means "to feel into" or "to feel with." Most of us have had the experience of sitting in the passenger's seat of a car and suddenly pushing a foot on the floor when we sense that the driver needs to put on the brakes. At such times we are feeling into the situation or feeling with the driver. To use more technical language, we are empathizing with the person who sits in the driver's seat.

In counseling and other forms of people helping, the helper shows empathy when he or she tries to see and understand a problem from the other person's perspective. Why is the person in front of me so upset? we might ask ourselves. How does she (or he) view the situation? If I were struggling with this problem, how would I feel? As helpers we try to keep our objective viewpoints intact, but we also know that there is value in trying to see the problem from the helpee's point of view. If we can communicate this, the helpee feels more understood and realizes that the helper really is trying to understand. This mutual sensitivity builds maximum rapport between the helper and the helpee. Good rapport, in turn, is a basis for effective helping.

Warmth is somewhat similar to caring. It is friendliness and consideration shown by facial expression, tone of voice, gestures, posture, eye contact, and nonverbal behavior that communicates concern. Warmth says, "I care about you and your well-being." Here, as in so much human behavior, actions speak louder than words. The helper who really cares about people won't have to advertise this concern verbally. Everyone will be able to see it.

Genuineness means that the helper's words are consistent with his or her actions. The helper tries to be honest with the helpee, avoiding any statements or behavior that could be considered phony or insincere. Someone has suggested that the truly genuine person has consistent values and attitudes, is spontaneous, aware of his or her own feelings, not impulsive or disrespectful, and not inclined to be defensive. Genuine people are willing to share of themselves and let others know what they are feeling.

Jesus showed empathy, warmth, and genuineness, and the successful Christian people helper must do the same. It is possible, however, that each of these can be overdone. We can show so much *empathy* that we lose our objectivity, so much *warmth* that the helpee feels smothered by our concern, and so much *genuineness* that we lose sight of the helpee's needs and problems. The helper, therefore, must frequently examine his or her own motives for helping. Since it is difficult to evaluate ourselves honestly, a good friend can often help us keep a more objective perspective. It is likely that some of our own needs are being met when we enter helping relationships, but more important is building a climate of warmth and caring where others are helped with their problems and struggles.

People-Helper Principle No. 2: The Helpee

The helpee's attitudes, motivation, expectations, and desire for help are also important. At some time most counselors have had the frustrating experience of trying to work with someone who is stubborn, uncooperative, or not interested in making any changes. To work with a rebellious teenager who has been sent to be "straightened out" or to counsel a depressed person who believes that he or she "will never get better—so why try?" is to work with a person whose attitude will have to change before real helping can occur. When the helpee has unrealistic expectations, does not want help, fails to see that a problem exists, has no desire to change, or lacks faith in the helper or the helping process, then your work is unlikely to be very successful—at least until the person's perceptions or attitudes change.

God created us with free wills, and it is no more possible to help an unwilling helpee grow psychologically than it is to help a disinterested nonbeliever grow spiritually. In people helping, as in disciple building, such resistance must be acknowledged and the helpee must be helped to see the value in making changes.

Counseling and similar forms of helping are ways of assisting others to change and grow, but growth is easiest when the helper and helpee work together on the task. In one sense the helpee is the best informed individual in the world when it comes to the problem situation. He or she knows how it feels, how similar problems have been handled in the past, and what has been tried and found to *not* work. The helper and helpee must both use this information together.

Of course, it should not be assumed that the person who needs help is always resisting in a stubborn manner. Sometimes people are afraid. It can be hard for a person to talk about failures or problems, and sometimes the helpee doesn't even know what is wrong. To tell someone else about your personal life can be risky because this could bring criticism or rejection. Sometimes people don't know what to expect if they talk about a problem, and they may be afraid that the helper will "see right through me" or "try to psychoanalyze me." Then there is the attitude of frustration or self-condemnation that some helpees feel because they haven't been able to solve problems on their own. All of these can interfere with the helping process. The helper's task, therefore, is to provide an atmosphere where the helpee can be free to "open up."

For best results, the helpee really must want to change, must expect that things will get better with the helper's assistance, and must show a willingness to cooperate even if the process is painful. Stated somewhat differently, it is important for the helpee to have an attitude of hope so that he or she believes that the counseling will bring genuine change.

Several years ago a researcher studied a number of therapies, looking for features that might be common in them all.[4] He concluded that they all offer at least three benefits: a new perspective on oneself and the world, an empathic and trusting relationship with a counselor who cares, and hope for demoralized people. Many of the people whom we seek to help are anxious, discouraged, frustrated, and overwhelmed. They need to believe that things can and will get better. Small groups often provide this sense of hope, and so do relationships with a caring helper.

Jesus emphasized the value of hope and faith in his helping ministry. He commended the hemorrhaging woman for a faith that restored her health (Mark 5:34). He healed two blind men because of their faith (Matt. 9:29). And he cured an epileptic boy whose father believed in the Master's powers (Mark 9:23-27). In contrast, when Jesus was in his hometown, not many people were helped because they didn't believe in his healing powers (Matt. 13:58). It could be argued, perhaps, that faith as described in the Scriptures is different from hope and expectation, but they are linked by the writer of Hebrews (Heb. 11:1). Terms like *faith, hope, expectation,* and *belief* can be used somewhat interchangeably because they all convey the idea that when a helpee desires to improve and expects improvement, very often the person does get better—sometimes in spite of the helper and his or her techniques.

People-Helper Principle No. 3: The Relationship
The helping relationship between the helper and the helpee is of great significance. As every counseling student soon learns, good rapport is essential for effective helping—so essential that we might think of counseling as being a helping *relationship* between two or more people. Some research even suggests that the most essential predictor of counseling success is the relationship between the helper and the helpee. The better the relationship, the more likely are the results to be positive. Irvin D. Yalom writes, "The best research evidence available overwhelmingly supports the conclusion that successful therapy is mediated by a relationship between therapist and patient that is characterized by trust, warmth, empathic understanding, and acceptance."[5]

Helping relationships differ both in their nature and their depth. Sometimes the relationship involves sending help in the form of money or a note of encouragement, but more direct helping involves a closer (usually a face-to-face) relationship in which the participants work together on a problem or problems. When two people come together, they do not leave their personalities, values, attitudes, insecurities, needs, feelings, perceptions, and abilities at the door. All of these enter the relationship, and to the extent that people are different, each helping encounter is unique.

Consider, for example, how Jesus related to people. He didn't have the same kind of relationship with all of them.

With Nicodemus it was intellectual, with the Pharisees it often was confrontational, with Mary and Martha it was more relaxed, and with little children it was warm and loving. Jesus recognized individual differences in personality, needs, and level of understanding, and he treated people accordingly. When counselors try to treat all of their helpees in the same way, they fail to build good rapport because they are making the mistake of thinking that all people are alike. All people are *not* alike, and this must be recognized both in the relationships that we build and in the methods that we use.

Jesus not only dealt with people in different ways, but he also related to individuals at different levels of depth or closeness. John apparently was the closest. He was the disciple whom Jesus loved and perhaps the Master's nearest friend. Peter, James, and John together appear to have comprised an inner circle with whom Jesus had a special relationship. Although they were not as close as the inner three, the other disciples were Christ's constant companions, a band of twelve men who had been handpicked to carry on the work after the Lord's departure. In Luke 10 we read about a group of seventy-two who were given special training. Following the Resurrection he appeared to a larger gathering of five hundred people. At other times there were crowds, sometimes numbering in the thousands, many of whom may have seen Jesus only once and from a distance.

Most of us have these kinds of relationships with others. Some people are close, while others are farther removed. Consider, for example, the different degrees of closeness that a teacher might have with his or her students. For most of my career, I was a full-time teacher. As a follower of Jesus Christ, I felt an inescapable obligation to make disciples for the Master from among my students and helpees, but I approached these people in different ways, and I was closer to some than to others.

My graduate assistant usually was closest. I met with him almost daily. He worked for me part-time, helped me with my courses and research, and studied under my direction. At times we prayed together, shared our concerns together, and had lunch together. Often my assistant would visit in our home and observe as I relaxed or related to my family. At other times, he would see me under the pressure of trying to handle some problem or meet some deadline. We would talk at times about his conflicts and problems, but I also was open about my personal concerns and struggles. Over the years I have kept in contact with many of these people (I had a different graduate assistant every couple of years) even though I rarely see any of them now that they have moved and gone on with their careers. For a while, though, they interacted closely with an older Christian and learned how to teach others some of the things they learned from me.

As a professor, however, there were other students whom I met frequently, sometimes in little groups, but the contact was not as frequent and the discussion was more superficial than the conversations with my assistant. More distant was my relationship with those seventy or eighty students who enrolled in my classes each quarter. Even less involved was my contact with the whole student body, some of whom met me casually on campus or heard me speak in chapel but had no other contact. Then there are people who have heard me speak at some conference or read something I have written (like this book) but have had no personal contact.

In a helping relationship, two people may be very close, sometimes with even a two-way sharing of emotions, concerns, and needs. On other occasions the relationship is not as deep. Perhaps the helpee and helper see each other only once, talk about the helpee only, or chat about a relatively minor problem. It even is possible for the helper to help others from a distance—by writing a letter, teaching a class, or publishing a magazine article. Sometimes, we help people on a one-to-one basis in a formal setting, sometimes we work in a group, on occasion we talk on the street or next to a busy highway, or we may give help to people whom we have never met face-to-face.

Every helper-helpee relationship is in some sense unique. Each relationship depends on the personality of the people involved, the nature of the problems being considered, the depth of the discussion, and the psychological closeness of the helper to the person being helped. As we are about to see, helping must involve more than a relationship. It must start with a relationship. In general, the better the relationship, the more effective the helping.

People-Helper Principle No. 4:
Feelings, Thoughts, and Actions

Helping must focus on the helpee's emotions, thoughts, and behavior—all three. Successful helping involves more than a relationship between two sensitive people. Helping involves skills and techniques, which good counselors and others learn, practice, and constantly refine. It is true, of course, that some people seem to have an innate "feel" for helping. Apparently they are successful without training or knowledge of techniques. But even these people can be more effective when they learn to be aware of what the helpee feels, what he or she is thinking, and how the helpee's actions may be creating or influencing the problem.

When we look into Scripture, we see that feeling, thinking, and behavior are all of great—perhaps equal—importance.

Consider the *emotions*. Jesus himself wept on at least two occasions and sometimes got angry. He did not deny feelings, and neither did he condemn people for experiencing and expressing their emotions. Clearly he was sensitive to the feelings of others, such as his sorrowing mother at the time of the Crucifixion or the parents who brought their children to see the Lord but were rebuffed by the overprotective disciples. It is possible to overemphasize feelings in a counseling relationship, but it also is possible to stifle or deny them. Jesus did neither.

There were times, however, when he put more emphasis on rational *thinking*. Thomas was inclined to doubt, but Jesus dealt with these questions in a rational way. He did not ignore the intellectual concerns of Thomas or criticize him for a lack of faith. Instead, when the disciple doubted, Jesus supplied the evidence. Following the Resurrection, Thomas said, in essence, "I won't believe unless I can see with my eyes and touch the hands of Jesus with my fingers." As they met later, the Lord said to Thomas, "Put your finger here; see my hands. Reach out your hand and put it into my side. Stop doubting and believe" (John 20:27). In a similar way, when John the Baptist doubted during his last days in prison (Matt. 11:2-6), Jesus provided the rational facts that were needed. On numerous occasions he carried on intellectual debates with the religious leaders of his day. Probably the best known example was his discussion of theology and apologetics with Nicodemus in a debate that may have gone far into the night.

But Jesus also was very concerned about *behavior*. He told the woman taken in adultery to change her behavior and to sin no more. He instructed Martha to change her hectic lifestyle, he advised the rich young ruler to be less selfish, and he told two quarreling brothers to stop being so greedy. In talking with the Jews he stated that "if anyone chooses to do

God's will, he will find out whether my teaching comes from God" (John 7:17). Jesus knew that insight doesn't always come before we act; often we have to change behavior, obey, and take action first. Then we get insight. In his sermons and discussions with individuals the Lord repeatedly confronted people with their sinful, self-centered behavior and instructed them to change.

This emphasis on emotions, thinking, and behavior is seen in the book of Acts and on through the New Testament epistles. Frequently, believers are held responsible for their own actions, but there is never a hint of overemphasizing behavior to the exclusion of feeling and thinking.

At the end of his Letter to the Philippians, the apostle Paul gives practical advice for daily living, advice that applies equally well to developing good mental health. First, he deals with emotions. "Rejoice in the Lord always. I will say it again: Rejoice!" The apostle reminds us that the Lord is near and that we can present our requests to God, "by prayer and petition, with thanksgiving." With this realization, we need not be anxious about anything, and we can

Table 2-1 **Thinking, Feeling, Actions**

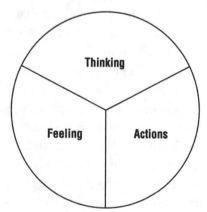

experience "the peace of God, which transcends all under-standing" (Phil. 4:4-7). Then there is an emphasis on think-ing. "Whatever is true, whatever is noble, whatever is right, whatever is pure, whatever is lovely, whatever is admirable—if anything is excellent or praiseworthy—think about such things" (Phil. 4:8). Finally there is emphasis on behavior. We should practice what we have learned and seen modeled in spiritual leaders like Paul. All of this should be done "through him who gives [us] strength" (Phil. 4:9-13).

Feeling, thinking, and behaving—all three are important in the Scriptures, and each must be considered in people helping. As shown in Table 2-1, each is in contact with the other. When we have emotional problems, for example, our thinking and actions are affected. We cannot emphasize one part while we ignore the other two. Most often, when people need help, they begin by talking about their feelings, such as sadness, discour-agement, loneliness, or anxiety. We can often help them change their feelings by helping them change their ways of thinking and behaving.

To this point we have seen four basic principles for helping others. But we have said very little about what we actually do when somebody asks for help. That is the focus of the next chapter.

Notes

1. The book *The Christian Psychology of Paul Tournier* (Grand Rapids: Baker, 1973) has been out of print for several years.
2. In using this term, I am not proposing any systematic approach or "new" school of counseling. I suggested the term when the first edition of this book appeared in 1976. Subsequent writers have used "discipleship counseling" in different ways, but I continue to think of this as a general summary term to describe what Christians do in their people helping. I have never attempted to formulate a "Collins" theory of counseling, and I have neither the inclination nor any plans to do this in the future.

3. Much of this research is summarized in an excellent book by Siang-Yang Tan, *Lay Counseling: Equipping Christians for a Helping Ministry* (Grand Rapids: Zondervan, 1990). The classic research on counselor characteristics was done by R. R. Carkhuff and C. B. Truax. Initially this attracted considerable attention, but interest subsequently faded. See C. B. Truax, "Therapist Empathy, Genuineness and Warmth, and Patient Therapeutic Outcome," *Journal of Consulting Psychology* 30 (1966): 395–401. Despite the controversy that still surrounds the Carkhuff-Truax work, I have decided to summarize it. A more contemporary perspective is discussed briefly in Catherine M. Flanagan in her book *People and Change* (Hillsdale, N.J.: Lawrence Erlbaum, 1990).

4. H. H. Strupp, "Psychotherapy: Research, Practice, and Public Policy: How to Avoid Dead Ends," *American Psychologist* 41 (1986): 120–30.

5. Irvin D. Yalom, *The Theory and Practice of Group Psychotherapy*, third ed. (New York: Basic Books, 1985), 48–49. Yalom cites some of the research that supports the crucial nature of the helping relationship. See, for example, S. Garfield and A. E. Bergin, eds., *Handbook of Psychotherapy and Behavior Change: An Empirical Analysis*, second ed. (New York: Wiley, 1978), 233–329.

CHAPTER THREE

The Techniques of People Helping

IN THE MIDST of some missionary activities in Bolivia, Henri Nouwen was asked if he would go to a cemetery to pray with a woman whose sixteen-year-old son, Walter, had died one month before. The woman was waiting on a bench in the village square of Cochabamba. The tears flowed freely as she told her sad story.

Walter had been riding on a truck filled with produce and people. As usual, the younger boys were standing on the running board, but at one point, Walter lost his balance. He fell between the wheels and was crushed by the back tires of the truck. Before they could get him to the hospital, the young man died.

When Nouwen stood with the grieving mother, next to the grave of her son, he felt overwhelmed by his inability to do anything. "I couldn't keep my eyes from the woman's face, a gentle and deep face that had known much suffering," he wrote later. "When I stood in front of the grave, I had a feeling of powerlessness and a strong desire to call Walter back to life. 'Why can't I give Walter back to his mother?' I asked myself. But then I realized that my ministry lay more in powerlessness than in power; I could only give her my tears." [1]

Sometimes, people helping leaves us feeling powerless—and maybe overwhelmed with tears. Confronted with deep sadness and human need, we often don't know what to do. Even Paul the apostle must have felt that way at times. Often he sensed his own frailties and inadequacies, but he knew that God uses and strengthens us when we feel weak. "I came to you in weakness and fear, and with much trembling," Paul wrote to his fellow believers at Corinth (1 Cor. 2:3-4). "My message and my preaching were not with wise and persuasive words, but with a demonstration of the Spirit's power." Later he wrote, "When I am weak, then I am strong" (2 Cor. 12:10).

Paul never used his weakness as an excuse for not studying or for being unprepared. He was a student of God's Word. He was well aware of the thinking and learning of the culture in which he lived. He knew about personal struggles, and he was sensitive to the needs of people in his society.

Like Paul, all servants of Christ feel weak and powerless at times, but we recognize that Christ gives us strength and wisdom when we need it most. We know, too, that he expects us to study and to learn all we can about the work that we are doing. This brings us to the next principle for Christian people helpers.

People-Helper Principle No. 5: Skills

Helping involves a variety of skills that need to be learned. Numerous books have been written to describe counseling techniques. Some estimates suggest that more than three thousand counseling methods currently exist, and the lists vary from author to author. Most counselors would agree, however, that in order to understand and help another human being, the helper must at least make use of the following basic helping skills.

Attending

Can you imagine what it would be like to go for counseling, burdened with some problem, only to find that the counselor sorts through the morning mail while you talk? Probably you wouldn't go back. Who wants to talk about personal issues with a helper who gets distracted and doesn't pay attention?

Several years ago, a University of Massachusetts psychologist named Allen Ivey developed a highly acclaimed method for teaching people to counsel.[2] The approach had twelve steps, all beginning with something called "attending behavior." This involves paying close attention to the helpee, encouraging him or her to talk freely, and showing by your actions that you are listening and not being distracted by other things.

According to Ivey, attending involves at least four behaviors: First, there is *eye contact.* As you talk and listen, look at the helpee. Second, show *attentive body language.* People know you are interested if you face them squarely, lean a little forward in your seat, appear relaxed, and show by your facial expressions and periodic head nods that you are paying attention. Third, *verbal qualities,* such as your tone of voice, pitch, volume, and rate of speech, are important. Then there is what Ivey calls *verbal tracking*—staying with the topic that the helpee presents and resisting the temptation to change the subject or to ask irrelevant questions. Sometimes you will notice that a helpee changes the subject especially when he or she is not comfortable. Gentle suggestions or brief comments can get the discussion back on track.

The goal in all of this is to enable the helpee to feel relaxed and able to share. Remember, you can't learn about the person or the problem if you are doing most of the talking. Instead, try to make encouraging statements ("That makes sense" or "I can see what you mean"), an occasional probing response ("Go on," "Tell me more," or "What then?"), and a periodic repeating of what the helpee has said, just to be sure that you understand.

If you find that you do talk too much (many of us do), ask yourself why. Often we talk too much when we feel uncomfortable or don't know what to say. Encouraging the helpee to talk and paying attention can be important starting places in people helping. Then, as the person talks, we can listen.

Listening

Jesus listened patiently (Luke 24:13-24), even though he had perfect knowledge of the personalities and problems of the people with whom he spoke. By his listening, Jesus was perhaps showing the therapeutic value of letting an individual put his or her troubles into words that can be shared with another (James 5:16).

When we listen, we are better able to understand others and their problems. But listening does more. It builds rapport with the helpee, shows that we care, and demonstrates that we really are interested and willing to share the burdens of another (Gal. 6:2; James 1:19). Often the very act of listening can be helpful because this gives the other person an opportunity to talk freely about a problem and to express in words what he or she has been feeling and thinking.

Table 3-1 gives some general guidelines for making your listening more helpful to others. As you read this table and

Table 3-1 Guidelines for Effective Listening

1. *Prepare to listen.*	Sometimes you have no prior warning before some person talks about a problem, but when there is time to prepare, try to get ready physically and mentally.
	Physically, recognize that listening is hard work, so try to get enough rest before you meet with a helpee. Sit in a relaxed posture as you listen, but don't be too casual. This can induce fatigue or grogginess and can give the impression that you are not taking the helpee's problems seriously.
	Mentally, try to prepare by reading about the issue that will be discussed. Informed listeners can often be more sensitive and able to listen better.
2. *Check your listening attitudes.*	Remember the following:
	• When you want to listen and recognize the importance of listening, you will listen more effectively.
	• Listening is one of the best ways to learn new information and ideas, but it also is one of the best ways to learn about people. The more we listen, without jumping to conclusions, the clearer our understanding.
	• Concentration is not easy; listening requires discipline.
	• Listening is as important as speaking. A poor listener is likely to be a poor speaker as well (James 1:19).
	• Even quiet times are significant—especially if we avoid the temptation to break the silence with talk. Often people need time to think, and silence allows this—even though it may leave everyone feeling uncomfortable.
	• When we learn to listen to others, we often are better able to listen to God.

Table 3-1 Guidelines for Effective Listening *(cont.)*

3. Be aware of both content and delivery.	What the speaker says is important, but how he or she communicates is also significant. Look for evidence of tears, trembling, posture shifts, change in voice pitch or speed, alterations in breathing rate. Notice when these occur. Often such nonverbal signs indicate that the person is talking about an especially significant or sensitive topic.
4. Be aware of your own emotions.	At times you might feel overpowered, angry, threatened, or sad. Don't stop listening because you feel uncomfortable or dislike what you are hearing. Ask yourself why you are responding in the way you are. Be patient as the other person talks.
5. Resist distractions.	You can be distracted by what you hear, by what you see, and by your wandering mind. Try to resist these distractions. Think about why you are getting distracted.
6. Encourage further sharing.	Head nods, a phrase such as "uh-huh," an occasional paraphrasing or repetition of what the helpee said, a short "tell me more" comment—all of these can encourage the other person to keep talking. This sharing is likely to continue if your posture and facial expressions show that you are interested.
7. Remember, you can think faster than the other person can talk.	Because of this, you can reflect on what you are seeing and hearing, evaluate what you have heard, and ask yourself what the helpee really is trying to communicate (or what he or she may be trying to hide).
8. Ask questions sparingly— especially at the beginning.	Try to avoid asking the question *why.* This often distracts the person into giving explanations or justifications for behavior. This, in turn, often shifts attention away from more pressing and more emotional issues.

Table 3-1 Guidelines for Effective Listening *(cont.)*

9. *Try not to interrupt.*	
10. *Avoid preaching, lecturing, giving advice, or arguing.*	
11. *Listen for themes.*	Do some topics, phrases, or people's names come up repeatedly? These repetitions may be clues to significant issues.
12. *Don't get carried away by your own curiosity.*	Your purpose in listening is to understand and help the other person, not to satisfy your own curiosity, lusts, or personal needs.

as you listen, try to remember that effective helpers are not only concerned with hearing the words that are being said. We watch for facial expressions, tears, changes in tone of voice, expressions of emotion, shifts in posture, and other clues that let us understand better. We want to hear what the helpee says, but we also want to learn something about his or her feelings, point of view, attitudes, and expectations.

As you listen and observe, it is often helpful to ask yourself some questions. For example, you might ask, "Is what I am hearing the real problem, or is there really another issue?" Ask yourself what details are being left out of the story that you are hearing. What might the person really be saying by his or her behavior and words? The goal is not to distrust the helpee. We don't want to snoop, like Sherlock Holmes, for clues that might uncover something hidden. But often what we see and hear may be an expression of something deeper.

Every parent knows that the cry of a baby means "I am

uncomfortable," but the parent's job is to discover the reason. Nurses often discover that constant demands from difficult patients sometimes mean "I feel out of control and don't know what to do," or "I'm afraid." Sometimes listeners have to look behind what we see or hear to discover what really is being expressed.

Listening, therefore, is not a passive activity that we do halfheartedly while our minds and attention wander. Counseling books often refer to *active* listening because effective listening takes intense concentration and careful attention.

An unwillingness to do the work of listening can be a great obstacle to helping. This is true in evangelism and discipleship as well as in counseling. If you are always talking, you won't understand the other person's needs, struggles, and questions. If you are too quick to give advice and answers, you are likely to undermine your own attempts to be a helper. Wise King Solomon once wrote that it is foolish to give answers before listening (Prov. 18:13).

I once met a counselor who didn't like to listen because he didn't want to be "a garbage pail getting filled with details of the junk and sinful behavior in other people's lives." I can understand my friend's concern. There is a place for innocence and purity on the part of the helper (Matt. 10:16; 1 Cor. 14:20), and it is neither helpful nor edifying to develop an expertise in understanding the details of other people's sins. Sometimes, therefore, you may need to say, "I think I'm getting the picture, so you probably don't need to repeat all the details of the situation." Be careful, however, that you don't intervene with such a statement too quickly. It could stifle discussion and cut you off from information that might be beneficial in your helping. Incidentally, my friend who complained about being a garbage pail is no longer a counselor. When he stopped listening, he stopped being helpful.

Leading

Sometimes we use techniques that encourage helpees to talk. We may want them to share feelings, to say what they are thinking, or to describe what has been done or not done about the problem in the past. On occasion, however, they clam up and seem uncomfortable, unwilling, or unable to talk. Perhaps there are few things more frustrating, especially for the novice counselor, but you might try some of the following to stimulate conversation. These approaches can also be used to stimulate the thinking and comments of helpees who don't talk freely but who may benefit from our prompting them to look at issues from a fresh perspective.

- Ask a question or make a request that can *not* be answered by a single word, such as a simple yes or no. For example, say, "Tell me what you are thinking about right now." "Tell me more about your parents." "Give me an example of what you mean by not getting along with your boss."
- Give a periodic brief summary of the situation as you see it, and ask if your perception is correct. If not, ask the helpee to correct your summary.
- Try a leading comment. These are statements designed to keep the conversation going. "What happened next?" you might ask. "Where did you go from there?" "What do you think will happen now?"
- Use a technique that psychologists call *reflecting*. This involves saying in fresh words what the helpee seems to be expressing or feeling. Examples: "That must have made you feel pretty good!" "Sounds to me like you feel guilty about what you did." "I gather her comment really made you mad."

- Restate the helpee's thoughts. This is another type of reflection and might include statements such as "Am I picking up that you're not sure of yourself on a date?" "Does what you have been saying mean that you don't know how to talk to your teenager?" "I get the impression that you are confused by what your boss is telling you."
- Offer a description of the helpee's behavior as you see it. Sometimes these are called *immediacy responses* because they give the helper's perception of what is happening immediately, right now. For example, say, "Right now you seem to be pretty tense." "You're smiling, but I get the idea that you really hurt inside."

After any of these responses, the helpee should be given the opportunity to respond—even if this consists of him or her telling you that you have missed the point completely. In using these leading responses, our goal is to encourage helpees to state their feelings and thoughts and to look honestly at behavior. This enables us to get information and to correct our misperceptions. More important, it helps the helpee get a clearer perspective on his or her problem. Then the person can be helped to get new insights or to change behavior and thinking.

Jesus used leading comments when he walked with those two discouraged followers on the road to Emmaus. "What are you discussing together as you walk along?" he asked. When the two stood still, their faces downcast, Jesus must have noticed the nonverbal behavior. Cleopas, one of the two, then referred to "the things" that had happened recently in Jerusalem. "What things?" Jesus asked. These were excellent leading questions that got them talking (Luke 24:17-19).

Supporting

Few biblical parables are better known than the story that
Jesus told about a Good Samaritan (Luke 10:30-37). When
he was found at the side of the road, severely beaten by rob-
bers, the injured man needed to be supported and taken to a
place where medical treatment and recuperation were possible. Jesus told his hearers to "go and do likewise."

We do something similar when we support people through
times of crises or psychological and spiritual injury. The word
support in no way implies that the helper holds up psychological cripples so that they never learn to face or to cope with
their problems. Even the Good Samaritan got the injured
man to the inn, helped him on the road to recovery, and then
left. We are not called to be rescuers whose personal self-
esteem depends on our unhealthy needs to have others be dependent on us.

There are times, however, when all of us need another person to lean on. During these periods of special need, a supportive friend or counselor can give encouragement, help,
guidance, and sometimes tangible assistance. When they give
spiritual and psychological support, people helpers recognize
that it is difficult for any of us to open up, to talk about failures, to admit sinful thoughts and actions, or to acknowledge
that some problem has us defeated. To talk openly—especially to another Christian—is to risk being rejected, criticized, or ostracized. This is why people often keep their
failures and inner thoughts to themselves. If we tell others,
they might think less of us or even turn away from us. This
fear of criticism or rejection causes many people to put up a
front before others so they can't see what we really are like.
Because of this, the person behind the mask fails to get the
personal support that could be a healing balm.

The Bible tells us that we should confess our faults, not

only to God in prayer, but also to one another (James 5:16). In hearing such confessions our reaction must not be shock or condemnation, but neither do we condone sinful behavior or pretend that it is unimportant. The Christian sympathetically bears the helpee's burdens (Rom. 15:1; Gal. 6:2). At times we rejoice with others over some victory, but at other times we weep together (Rom. 12:15). If there is sin, we encourage the helpee to confess it, and we stay nearby offering comfort and help as the person works to change his or her attitudes and behavior. By doing this, we are giving emotional and spiritual support as the helpee takes steps toward greater personal maturity and growth.

Influencing

It is possible for the helper to listen, to make leading comments, and to support the helpee who, nevertheless, doesn't get better at all. This is because the helpee's problem is rooted in behavior, attitudes, or thoughts that must be changed. For such change to occur, the person with the problem must face up to his or her actions, and the helper must guide this process along using a number of influencing techniques.

In one of his books on counseling, Jay Adams writes that all counselors hold one view in common. "No matter how divergent their dogmas, all counselors—Christians included—agree that the aim of counseling is to *change* people. Change—whether in the helpee's thinking, feeling, behavior, attitude, sensitivity, awareness, or understanding—is the goal of *all* counseling." [3]

How do we influence people so that they change? Table 3-2 lists a number of "influencing skills" that helpers might use with others. Notice that the list starts with methods by which the helper does not exert much influence over others

Table 3-2 **Influencing Skills**

1. *Restating, paraphrasing, summarizing*	Here the helper pulls together what has been said and repeats or restates this using different words. This lets the helpee see the problem in a new light.
2. *Giving feedback*	Sometimes there is a need for accurate data on how the helper or others view the person who has come for help. Try to be specific, nonjudgmental, informative. Remember that most people can accept only one piece of information like this at a time, so don't overwhelm. Give the helpee opportunity to respond. For example: "Mary, I wonder if you have noticed that every time I begin to talk, you interrupt me. I suspect that others feel frustrated like I do when we aren't able to get a word in edgewise."
3. *Making self-disclosures*	At times the helper expresses his or her thoughts or feelings to the helpee. It can be useful for the helpee to know how you are feeling, but be careful not to shift the focus of helping onto yourself or imply that your attitudes, emotions, or opinions are the only valid or correct ones. It is best to start your self-disclosure by using statements like "From my perspective . . . ," "I wonder if . . . ," "It seems to me that . . . ," or "Once I was in a somewhat similar situation when . . ."
4. *Making suggestions, giving advice, or providing information*	Sometimes others need guidance, information, or skills that will help them deal with issues more effectively. It is best to be respectful and gentle in giving advice, guidance, information, or suggestions. Helpers often give advice without listening first. There is often a tendency to tell people what to do—especially when we aren't sure what else to say. In turn, the recipients of this information often resist being told how to change, and frequently

Table 3-2 **Influencing Skills** *(cont.)*

<table>
<tr>
<td></td>
<td>such advice is ignored.

Try, instead, to give information in the form of suggestions. For example, "How would you feel about talking directly to your boss about the way you are being treated?" or "I have some suggestions that might help you to study more effectively." Give the helpee opportunity to agree, disagree, or respond in other ways.</td>
</tr>
<tr>
<td>5. Making interpretation</td>
<td>Here the helpee is given a different and unique way of looking at some issue. Be tentative as you present your interpretations about what is going on; you could be wrong. For example, "John, I noticed that most of the problems you have mentioned revolve around issues of authority. I wonder if these problems all show a tendency in you to resist any person who is in authority?"</td>
</tr>
<tr>
<td>6. Stating logical consequences</td>
<td>This is a method by which the helper states what is likely to happen if the helpee continues on his or her present course of action. Once again, try not to use these statements as hammers intended to force change. Words of manipulation almost always bring resistance. For example, instead of saying, "You had better cut this out or you're going to be on the street," it usually is better to say, "As you are smart enough to know, if this workaholic lifestyle persists, you could be successful in your career but lose your family." These statements of logical consequences can lead to discussions about how the helpee might change.</td>
</tr>
<tr>
<td>7. Giving directives and making confrontations</td>
<td>This involves telling the helpee what he or she must do to change. Often this involves pointing out the inconsistencies, sinful relationships, or other attitudes and behaviors that need to be changed.</td>
</tr>
</table>

and moves to techniques, like confrontation, that are more directive.

It is unlikely that you would use all of these techniques with one person, and it may be that you won't use some of these techniques at all. Some people, for example, are gentle by nature and not very confrontive, even when confrontation might be needed. Others are like one of my counselor friends who is very compassionate and sensitive to people but whose personality and manner is such that he can be very confrontive in a way that nobody feels put down or disrespected.

All of these techniques can influence other people to change. Ultimately, however, change must come as the Holy Spirit works within the lives of the helpee and helper, and as he guides the helping relationship toward behavior and attitudes that are consistent with the teachings of God's Word. I agree that whatever the person's problems may be, "there can be no change that is acceptable to God, and in the long run, to the helpee, until fundamental, positive change toward God has occurred. . . . The Christian counselor is to minister God's Word in a life-transforming way, such that God himself changes the helpee—from the heart outward." [4]

Confronting

Confrontation has become a controversial topic in Christian helping. Following the lead of the person-centered (nondirective) therapies, many pastoral counselors and other Christian helpers work on the assumption that confrontation is rarely needed, if at all, and that usually it is ineffective. Others argue that to be competent and genuinely Christian, counselors almost always must confront people with their failures to live in accordance with the Word of God.

Jesus did a great deal of confrontation. He confronted the Pharisees with their hypocrisy, the disciples with their lack of understanding, Martha with her excessive busyness, and the rich young ruler with his misplaced values. It seems, in fact, that confrontation was a major way by which Jesus dealt with others. It was a technique that was carried into the early church and was seen most clearly when Paul confronted Peter with his cowardly capitulation to the demands of people who were known as Judaizers (Gal 2:1-21).

Confrontation involves pointing out sin in another person's life but is not limited to this. We can confront helpees with their inconsistent behavior ("You say you love your wife, but you are mean to her"; "You claim to like sports but you never play"); with their self-defeating behavior ("You want to succeed, but you set your standards so high that you are sure to fail"); or with their tendencies to evade issues ("You say you want to grow spiritually, but every time this issue comes up you change the subject").

Confrontation is a difficult task. To be most effective in bringing change, it is best done in a gentle and nonjudgmental fashion (Matt. 7:1; Gal. 6:1). The helper must be courageous enough to risk getting overt or passive resistance from the helpee who might not want to face the reality of his or her sin, failure, or inconsistency in life. Remember that your task is not to condemn but to help, not to stir up trouble but to stimulate healing. Sometimes healing must be preceded by painful surgery, but to be successful this must not come until there has been a building of trust in the "surgeon."

When you see the need to confront, also try to give support. The helpee is likely to feel threatened when he or she is confronted, so you might say, for example, "Susan, I really value our relationship, but because of that, I think I need to share something difficult. . . ." Be sure to give ample opportunity for the confronted person to respond, either by expressing his or her reaction to the confrontation or by changing behavior. In helping, think of yourself and your helpee as working together on a problem, more or less as a team of equals. You are not a counselor-judge who lords it over a helpee-victim.

Teaching

Counseling and other forms of people helping are specialized types of teaching. The person in need is learning how to act, feel, and think differently; the helper is fulfilling the role of a teacher.

Teaching, of course, can occur in a variety of ways. It may involve instruction, giving advice, or telling others what to do. Very often, however, such verbal direction has little impact. It usually is more effective for helpers to show by their behavior and lifestyles how to live or think more effectively; to give praise, encouragement, or other reinforcement when a helpee shows improvement; and to work with helpees as they make decisions, take actions, and evaluate what they are doing to change. Sometimes it helps to do role plays in which one person practices new behavior in the presence of another person who gives guidance and feedback. For example, an insecure young man might practice ways of asking for a date, or a nervous businessman might practice his sales proposal before his coworkers before presenting the proposal to a prospective client.

All of these techniques describe what the counselor-helper can do, but equally important is the question of goals. Where is the people helping going, and what does it seek to accomplish? This leads to our next principle.

People-Helper Principle No. 6: Disciple Making

The ultimate goal of helping is to make disciples and disciplers of the people whom we help. This statement could be greatly misunderstood and highly criticized. It seems to imply that helping is concerned only with spiritual matters or that the most important goal is to get people converted rather than helping them with their needs and problems.

People helping can have a variety of goals, depending on the problem and the person who is being helped. The helper, for example, may

1. seek to change the helpee's behavior, attitudes, or values;
2. teach social skills;
3. encourage the expression of emotions;
4. give encouragement and support;
5. confront sin, inconsistencies, and other forms of self-harming behavior;
6. instill insight, guide as a decision is made;
7. teach responsibility;
8. provide financial or other forms of tangible assistance;
9. stimulate spiritual growth;
10. resolve interpersonal conflict; or
11. help an individual mobilize his or her inner resources in times of crisis.

That is an impressive list—and it probably isn't complete. How, then, do we conclude that disciple making is the ultimate goal of people helping?

Think for a moment about the Christian physician. Like every other believer, he or she too has a responsibility to be making disciples, but in the emergency room the competent doctor does not pull out a Bible and start preaching. Like Jesus, the doctor starts with people where they are hurting. Through the skilled use of medical procedures, the physician demonstrates Christian love, realizing that the alleviation of suffering is honoring to Christ and often a first step toward evangelism (Prov. 14:31; Matt. 10:42). The physician does not avoid talk about spiritual matters, but this is not the major part of treatment. At some time, the doctor hopes that there will be opportunity to discuss spiritual as well as medical issues.

In the discipling process there are at least five steps. We must make contact, witness verbally with our words and non-verbally by our actions, bring persons to the point of conversion, help them to grow as disciples, and teach them how to disciple others. This has several implications for people helping.

First, the helper may come into a life at any point in these five steps. He or she may deal with a nonbeliever who has never heard the gospel, or counsel with a mature saint who has been growing as a disciple and discipler for many years. Some Christian counselors have suggested that we must restrict our people helping to believers, but the Bible teaches otherwise. "As we have opportunity, let us do good to *all* people, especially to those who belong to the family of believers" (Gal. 6:10, emphasis added).

Second, there may be times when you take a person through all five stages, but more often you will be with a helpee for a short time, have some influence in his or her life, and then move out while another person takes over. Sometimes one person makes contact and even does some counseling, another person witnesses, someone else leads the person to Christ, and then the discipling is taken over by still others. Often God uses a multitude of individuals to touch lives and to bring the help that is needed. This is illustrated in 1 Corinthians 3:4-10, where Paul recognized that discipleship may involve the mutual efforts of a number of believers. As helpers, we want to be among those who are used by God to touch the lives of our helpees. Our goal is not to be possessive of others so that we take over and do everything ourselves. Instead, we seek to be part of the long-term disciple-making process, intervening at the points where we can make the most needed impact.

Closely related is a third implication. Like discipleship in general, helping involves the whole body of Christ. In Romans 12, 1 Corinthians 12, and elsewhere in Scripture we read that believers exist in a body for mutual support, help, burden bearing, and edification. Perhaps we have settled too quickly and too rigidly into the idea that discipleship, counseling, and other forms of helping always involve a one-to-one type of relationship. Instead, the church must be a healing community that supports the work of individual helpers and the growth of helpees.

Fourth, recognize that just as spiritual issues too often are ignored, there also are times when the spiritual can be introduced too quickly and too abruptly. Some helpees have been turned off in the past by well-meaning but pushy Christians who have rushed in to condemn behavior, present the gospel, or give minisermons on how to live better lives. Instead, the helper must be sensitive to the Holy Spirit's leading. This may mean that spiritual things are not mentioned until later in the helping process and that sometimes they don't get mentioned at all. Often a low-key approach to discipleship is the best way to begin.

Finally, discipleship counseling is concerned about the whole person. Each human being is a unified individual. Rarely, if ever, does one have a strictly spiritual need, a solely psychological abnormality, an exclusively social conflict, or a purely physical illness. When something goes wrong with one aspect of the unified person, the individual's whole being is affected. A healer may specialize in medicine, psychotherapy, or spiritual counseling, but each must remember that there is no sharp line of division between the spiritual, emotional, volitional, or physical aspects of a person. One symptom may cry for healing, but at such time the entire body is off balance. We must not deal with the spiritual and forget the person's psychological or physical needs; they go together, and the helper who forgets this does the helpee and the Lord a disservice.

These, then, are the six principles of discipleship counseling and people helping. They concern the importance of the helper, the attitudes of the helpee, the helping relationship, the importance of feeling, thinking, and actions, the use of helping skills, and the goal of discipleship. We turn, now, to the process of helping. From this we will be able to see how these principles and our helping actions work out in practice.

Notes

1. Henri J. M. Nouwen, *Gracias! A Latin American Journal* (San Francisco: Harper & Row, 1983), 91.
2. Allen E. Ivey, *Intentional Interviewing and Counseling*, second ed. (Monterey, Calif.: Brooks/Cole, 1988).
3. Jay Adams, *How to Help People Change* (Grand Rapids: Zondervan, 1986), xi. See also Catherine M. Flanagan, *People and Change: An Introduction to Counseling and Stress Management* (Hillsdale, N.J.: Lawrence Earlbaum, 1990).
4. Adams, *How to Help*, 3, 7.

CHAPTER FOUR

The Direction of People Helping

THE BIBLE often mentions people helping, but perhaps no example is as clear as the help given by Jesus on the road to Emmaus (Luke 24:13-35). A few days after the Resurrection, two people were walking to a village about seven miles from Jerusalem. The travelers were confused about all that had happened, and they were talking about these events as they walked.

When Jesus approached and began walking with them, they didn't recognize who he was, and neither did they realize that he was using a variety of people-helping techniques to help them through their crisis and period of discouragement. Notice that the counseling in this situation did not take place in an office; there was no calling for an appointment, diploma on the wall, or fee. Jesus gave help on a dusty road as the three walked together late one afternoon.

At the beginning, *Jesus came alongside* the two perplexed individuals and began traveling with them. Here was rapport building—a showing of interest in their needs and a willingness to meet them where they were. Like Jesus, the helper today must be willing to go where helpees are. If you passively wait for people to come to you with their problems, your helping effectiveness is likely to be limited.

A few days after my mother died and we had returned from the funeral, the members of our Bible study group appeared one evening at our door. They brought food, cards, and love. As we sat around the table, I was amazed at the comfort I felt, being in the presence of these people who had "come alongside" in a time of stress and grief.

As he joined the two people in their journey, *Jesus began asking questions.* Usually we think of questions as being of two types, closed-ended and open-ended. Closed questions usually bring a one or two word answer. "Are you married?" is an example. Open-ended questions are more likely to get the person talking. Jesus asked two of these. "What are you discussing together as you walk along?" he asked. When one of them referred to the things that had been happening, Jesus asked, "What things?"

At that point they began talking, and *Jesus listened.* Since he already knew what was distressing them, he didn't learn anything new, and surely he didn't agree with their interpretation of recent events in Jerusalem. But he gave them opportunity to express their frustrations, and he demonstrated the love that had sent him to die for sinners. As they all walked, perhaps he made a few influencing statements to help keep the conversation moving.

After a period of time, *Jesus confronted* the two travelers with their logical misunderstandings and failure to understand the Scriptures. The confrontation was gentle but firm, and it must have begun the process of stimulating the two to change their thinking and behavior. Then *Jesus*

began to teach, explaining things from the Bible that concerned their problem. Today, centuries later, people helpers
still function as teachers, helping others to see their errors
and to learn how they might think or behave differently.

Near the end of the journey, *Jesus got close* by accepting an
invitation to have a meal with the two travelers. In any helping situation it is important to take the risk of getting near
to those we help emotionally and psychologically. But we
need to be careful. In a later chapter we will consider some
problems that can arise when we get too close to the people
who look to us for help.

Probably you remember that the trip to Emmaus had an
unusual ending. It was something that every helper would
like to have happen at some time—especially when the
helping relationship is difficult. Jesus disappeared from
their sight. In so doing, he was not abandoning his helpees.
Instead, *Jesus left them on their own and spurred them to
action.* This is the ultimate goal of helping—to move
others to a point of independence where there is no longer
a need to rely on the help of the helper.

Notice how the two disciples responded after they realized
that Jesus had been their counselor. Before rushing back to
Jerusalem, "they asked each other, 'Were not our hearts burning within us while he talked with us on the road and opened
the Scriptures to us?'" They had not recognized who he was,
but Jesus had made a powerful impact, especially through his
use of the Scriptures.

This has relevance for people helpers today. Jesus, of
course, has gone back to heaven, but his Holy Spirit is present in the lives of the Christians who remain here on earth.
When we yield to his control, the Holy Spirit guides our
people helping even though we may not be aware of his
presence. Sometimes, when we give help that is consistent

with the Scriptures, we sense the power of God "burning within us." The Creator of the universe doesn't leave us alone to be Christian people helpers.

As he helped people, Jesus used a variety of methods; what he did on the road to Emmaus is not the only way to be a people helper. With Nicodemus, for example, he sat and had a late-night, rational discussion about theology. He encouraged and supported the timid woman with the blood disorder, confronted the woman at the well with her immorality, directed the woman taken in adultery to sin no more, criticized the proud Pharisees in a very direct fashion, prepared his disciples for the future when he sent them out two by two, and served as a model of how one ought to live the Christian life.

Following in his steps, Christian people helpers must live lives that are in close fellowship with God. We must spend regular times in prayer and meditation on Scripture, shun sin in our daily life, and confess our transgressions when we fail. In working with others, we must meet them where they are, accept them as individuals to be loved even if their behavior is sinful and unlovely, seek at all times to be models of what God wants us to be, and use techniques that are consistent with Scripture. Our desire is to bring about behavior, thinking, and feelings that are in greater conformity with the Word of God.

At this point, it is important to give a word of caution. In each of the approaches that we have described to this point, including the counseling that was given by Jesus on the road to Emmaus, there is a lengthy period of listening and rapport building. In their enthusiasm and desire to be genuinely helpful, beginning counselors and other helpers often feel pressured to come up with answers, or they push their helpees to action. More often, there needs to be a long period of listening, understanding, and exploration before we start moving into solutions. This brings us to the process of helping.

The Helping Process

People helping can be very difficult. Despite our best efforts, sometimes others resist our help or refuse to cooperate. Often problems are deeply entrenched and so complicated that only the counseling expert knows what to do. Some professionals argue that genuine and permanent helping is a long process. According to these therapists, it is unrealistic to think that problems can be handled in a few minutes or a few hours when they may have taken years to develop.

Certainly many problems are complex and best left to the experts,[1] but even the experts admit that many issues can be resolved if we follow a systematic formula. In one of his excellent books on helping skills, for example, Gerard Egan presents a "problem-management" approach to helping that consists of three stages. Stage one involves identifying and clarifying the problem situation, stage two involves goal setting, and stage three guides as the helpee moves to take action.[2] Writing from a Christian perspective, Carol Lesser Baldwin proposes a similar—although more directive—approach. She suggests that level one of helping involves learning to listen, level two concerns "speaking the truth," and level three directs the helpee to action.[3] A professional counselor named Catherine Flanagan condenses a wealth of complex people-helping information into two stages: identifying the problems and planning changes.[4]

A lot of what we do in helping others will depend on the type of problem involved, the personalities of the helper and helpee, and the nature of their relationship.

As a general guideline, however, you might want to think of six steps in people helping.

STEP 1: *Building Rapport* between the helper and helpee. It is here that the helper's empathy, warmth, genuineness, and caring characteristics are of special importance (John 6:63; 16:7-13; 1 John 4:6).

STEP 2: *Clarifying the Issues,* often through the use of listening, leading, supporting, and gentle probing with open-ended questions. This is a process that should not be hurried. Try to find out what has been done in the past to handle the problem. Be aware of what the helpee is feeling, but try to find out, too, what he or she thinks now about the problem and what behavior may be contributing to the problem issue. All of this emphasizes the importance of exploring and understanding problems before looking for solutions (Rom. 8:26; James 1:19).

STEP 3: *Exploring Alternatives,* listing and discussing several possible actions that could be tried, one at a time. Sometimes this involves brainstorming with the helpee, with both of you making and evaluating possibilities that might be tried (John 14:26; 1 Cor. 2:13).

STEP 4: *Stimulating Change* by deciding what needs to be done and then doing it. This may involve confrontation, teaching, and the use of influencing skills. Helpees may need to agree that they will change their thinking and actions. Often this is the best way to change feelings. If several alternatives seem feasible, the helpee needs to choose one tentatively and start moving in that direction. And in all of this, the Christian helper and helpee must seek the guidance of the Holy Spirit (John 16:13; Acts 10:19-20; 16:16; Heb. 10:24).

STEP 5: *Evaluating Results* to determine whether a course of action is working and whether it should be tried again or done in a different way.

STEP 6: *Terminating the Relationship* and encouraging helpees to apply what they have learned as they launch out on their own (Rom. 8:14).

For me, it is helpful to think of this as forming a circle. Step one gets us into the circle—and continues to be important as we follow the arrows. Sometimes we have to keep following those solid arrows around the circle repeatedly before we can move to step six. Even then, in the future, we may need to enter the circle again. All of this is illustrated in Table 4-1. If you keep this model in mind, it can give direction to your helping activities.

To illustrate how this works, we will use the example of how people make decisions. Of course, problems are rarely this simple or this cognitive, but the example will help you plant the six steps in your mind.

Helping People Make Decisions

What do you think was the most important decision that Jesus ever made? We might not all agree on an answer to that question, but surely the choice of his twelve disciples was near the top of the list. Jesus planned to teach these men intensively and to leave with them the whole work of spreading the gospel and establishing the church. Surely he must have spent many hours in prayer before making his selection.

Making decisions is not easy—especially when the decisions are important and life changing. Wise King Solomon wrote about the importance of seeking the advice of advisors before making a significant decision to act (Prov. 11:14; 15:22; 20:18). At times you will be the one who seeks advice from another individual or group of counselors; but sometimes another person will come to you for guidance. What do you do then?

Table 4-1

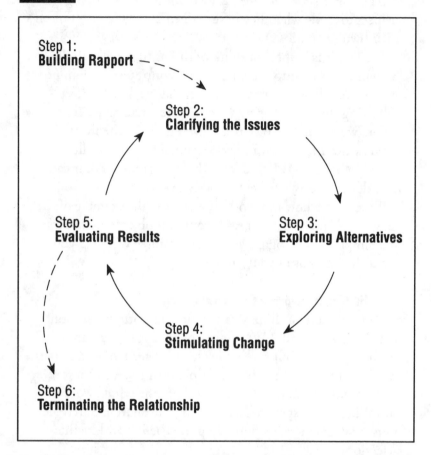

Step 1:
Building Rapport

Step 2:
Clarifying the Issues

Step 5:
Evaluating Results

Step 3:
Exploring Alternatives

Step 4:
Stimulating Change

Step 6:
Terminating the Relationship

When I go overseas on speaking trips, I like to have my
wife go with me, but if she cannot do this, I sometimes travel
with a student or another counselor. One time on a trip to
Tokyo, a young student accompanied me and mentioned on
the plane that he was debating about whether or not he and
his girlfriend should get married. As we traveled together we
had lots of time to talk, and I watched as my friend grappled
with his decision.

Look again at Table 4-1 again. Even if you and your helpee have a good relationship—like my student and I had a good relationship—continue to work on giving encouragement and support. That is *step one.* Remember that your job is *not* to say what should be done or to make a decision for the other person—even if you are convinced of what he or she should do. Your job, instead, is to guide, encourage, make occasional suggestions, and stick with the person through the decision-making process.

In *step two* you ask the person to clarify the issues. What is the decision that has to be made? Is there a time limitation for this? My friend who was struggling with a possible marriage had no time limitation—although he was a little worried lest his potential bride might get tired of waiting. There was a danger that she might get interested in somebody else.

Early in this clarification process you need to pray, asking God to give guidance and clear thinking. Continue to pray regularly as the helping process continues.

At some point you will shift into *step three* and begin listing alternatives. Many people find that this is best done on paper. If I am making an important decision, I often list the different alternatives, sometimes on separate pieces of paper. Then I jot down the positive points and the negative points for each alternative. Often I keep at this for several days or weeks. As more information becomes available, my listing of pros and cons tends to change and become clearer. Sometimes, in looking over what I have written, it becomes clear what should be done.

As my friend and I walked through some streets in Tokyo, he talked about the positives and negatives of marrying the girl he was dating. "Tell me," I said, "what are the advantages of marrying this girl?" He talked at some length about the girl's good points and the benefits of the marriage. After some time we stopped in a coffee shop, where I pulled out a pen and asked him to give me a list of the disadvantages of moving ahead with the marriage. He couldn't think of any! Suddenly it was clear to both of us that he had already made the decision (they had a beautiful wedding a few months later), but he had needed another person to help him think it through.

Most decisions are not that easy. Often after listing the alternatives and continuing to pray, the helper and helpee move to the *fourth step* of selecting the option that seems the best. Then the helpee starts moving tentatively in that direction. To fix this in your mind, you might think of decision making as a UPS delivery system in which you *U*nderstand the situation as best you can, *P*lan all of the alternatives, then *S*tep out in some kind of action. Having decided on a course of action, it is time to do something. Then you do it.

And what if this decision isn't right?

Probably you have heard the old saying that it is easier to steer a moving vehicle than one that is stopped and immobile. If we bathe our decision making in prayer, God often nudges us in directions that may be different from the course of action that we or our helpee took initially.

Even if he doesn't seem to lead us and we decide later that we have made the wrong move, we can evaluate where we went wrong (that's *step five*) and try again by moving in a different direction. If that isn't possible, we pick up and keep on going, confident that we made the wisest decision that we could, given all of the input that was available at the time.

Being a Mentor

Sometimes we help people in a less direct way, by being an example. Often others are watching us, and we don't even know it.

In writing to the Corinthians, Paul once made a startling statement: "Follow my example, as I follow the example of Christ" (1 Cor. 11:1). The apostle must have known what some of us have since discovered: People follow people. Kids tend to imitate parents (even when they don't like what the parents do), students imitate teachers, younger Christians become like those who are older, professional and business people who are starting their careers try to be like those who are successful and more established. Here is a statement that might make you feel uncomfortable: *It is probable that some individual or group of individuals is watching you and becoming like you.*

What is a mentor?

Within the past decade, the word *mentor* has regained popularity, perhaps because of some Yale researchers who described mentors in a popular book about adult development. More recently, Ted Engstrom, former president of World Vision, has written about mentoring from a Christian perspective. According to his definition, a mentor is someone, usually older than the protégé, who "provides modeling, close supervision on special projects, individualized help in many areas—discipline, encouragement, correction, confrontation, and a calling to accountability." [5] There are many biblical examples: Moses taught Joshua, Naomi taught Ruth, Elijah was a mentor to Elisha, Elizabeth guided Mary, Priscilla and Aquila taught Apollos, Barnabas taught Paul, who in turn taught Timothy. Unlike most of us, Jesus had a group of protégés—the disciples. He built them up, corrected them, challenged them, pushed them, trained them, and showed them how to live as followers of Christ. He was the perfect mentor. His life was a model of mentoring that we can follow in mentoring others.

69

It should not be assumed that all mentoring occurs in the same way. Sometimes, for example, there is more tutoring or guidance involved, while in other cases the mentor is more of a role model who is watched. Sometimes mentors and their protégés know each other well. At other times we have mentors whom we might not even have met.[6] Nevertheless, according to Engstrom, every Christian needs a mentor, a protégé, and a friend to enjoy on the peer level. The mentor, as you might suspect, gains as much as the protégé. When all of life is over, we might find that the most significant thing we ever did was to be a mentor, model, example, older friend, and encourager to people who are younger. That is a significant part of people helping.

Mentors and helpers

There are no rules for becoming a mentor, but there are some things you can do to get started.

First, think about the people who mentored you. I did this recently, writing down the names of individuals who had most influenced my life. Some I knew well; others were more like distant heroes whose lives I admired and whose actions I tried to follow—often unconsciously at the time. When you think about the people who most influenced you, it is possible to think how you, in turn, can best influence others.

Next, think of specific people who might be looking at you—perhaps even today—and following your example. Your protégés may be your children or other family members, people in your church, individuals where you work, or, if you teach, your students. Counseling books rarely imply that counselors should be mentors, but if you are a people helper, it is likely that some of the people who get help will look to you as a mentor.

While I was writing the preceding paragraphs, I was interrupted by a telephone call from a former student who told about a recent death in his family. During our conversation, he mentioned that for him, I had been a mentor whose example he had sought to follow. I was sobered by these words. His comments were a timely reminder of how others look to us as examples—especially in times of grief and struggle.

If you want to be a better mentor, try to follow Paul's example. He sought to be like Christ (1 Cor. 11:1). The younger believers who looked up to Paul must have known about his prayer life, his study of the Scriptures, and his consistent desire to serve the Lord. Good Christian mentors make it their business to become good Christians. Often God takes over and does the rest—leading you to people whom you might mentor and showing others that they should look to you.

If you want to be a mentor, ask God to lead you to some protégé—a person whom you can encourage and challenge, without smothering and overwhelming. The best mentors believe in their protégés, want them to succeed, rejoice with them when they are effective, do not get jealous of their accomplishments, pray for them consistently, call them to account on occasion, and become available to them—even when it isn't convenient.

In his letter to Timothy, Paul gives a good description of Christian mentoring. "Be strong in the grace that is in Christ Jesus. And the things you have heard me say in the presence of many witnesses entrust to reliable men who will also be qualified to teach others" (2 Tim. 2:1-2).

You can be a helper without being a mentor. Most of us do that often. But being a mentor is a special kind of people helping, a type of helping that is both demanding and highly rewarding.

Where do we start?

Some time ago I read about an electrician named Richard who was hired to do some work in an old building that was being remodeled for office space. Richard talked all the time, and after a while somebody started calling him "motor mouth." He had an opinion on every subject, but he also had a smile and was a likeable person, despite his constant chatter.

One day, about a year after the initial remodeling was complete, the building owners wanted to make some additional changes, so they called again to ask if Richard could do the wiring. But motor mouth, always laughing, always joking, always talking, was no longer available. One morning, after an argument, Richard had gone to the bedroom and returned to the kitchen where his wife was standing at the sink. He touched her on the shoulder, and she turned just in time to see Richard pull the trigger of the pistol that was pressed against his head.

"I'd asked him lots of times how he was doing," Bob Benson wrote later, "but I guess I never asked him in such a way that made him want to tell me."

Benson suggested that life, for many of us, is like those electric bumper cars at the amusement park. "We just run into each other and smile and bump and continue on our way."

"Hi, motor mouth." *Bump, bump!*

"How are you doing?" *Bump, bump!*

"I'm doing great, fantastic." *Bump, bump, bump!*

"And somebody slips out and dies because there is no one to talk to." *Bump, bump, bump.*[7]

Norman Cousins, long-time editor of the *Saturday Review,* once described how many of us feel when we think about the human need that surrounds us. Many of our mailboxes are filled with appeals from people who are needy. The homes in our neighborhoods hide incredible problems that cry out for attention but rarely get noticed. And behind every human being who cries out for help, Cousins has written, "there may be a million or more equally entitled to attention." Where, then, does one begin? How can we be sure that we don't miss the hurting "motor-mouths" who smile on the outside but hurt within? How do we choose where to give help?

Do not concern yourself with these questions. Norman Cousins suggests, "Reach out and take hold of the one who happens to be nearest. If you are never able to help or save another, at least you will have saved one."[8] We can create a lot of internal frustration, and sometimes plenty of interpersonal tension, if we get a rescue mentality that says we have to help everybody. Most of us will never change a whole society or a whole culture, but each of us can have an influence on the person or persons who are closest.

That, most often, is how we help: one person at a time—starting with the person who is nearest.

Notes

1. Please see chapter 8 for a discussion of how and when to make referrals to more experienced or better trained people helpers.
2. Gerard Egan, *The Skilled Helper: A Systematic Approach to Effective Helping,* fourth ed. (Monterey, Calif.: Brooks/Cole, 1994).
3. Carol Lesser Baldwin, *Friendship Counseling: Biblical Foundations for Helping Others* (Grand Rapids: Zondervan Pyranee Books, 1988).
4. Catherine M. Flanagan, *People and Change: An Introduction to Counseling and Stress Management* (Hillsdale, N.J.: Lawrence Erlbaum, 1990).
5. Ted W. Engstrom with Norman B. Rohrer, *The Fine Art of Mentoring: Passing On to Others What God Has Given to You* (Brentwood, Tenn.: Wolgemuth & Hyatt, 1989), 4.
6. The Search Institute (700 South Third Street, Suite 210, Minneapolis, MN 55415) has studied differing mentoring styles, especially as these relate to mentoring young people. See, for example, the November 1992 issue of Search Institute *Source,* for a brief article entitled "The Diversity of Mentoring."

7. Bob Benson and Michael W. Benson, *Disciplines for the Inner Life* (Waco, Tex.: Word, 1985), 312.
8. Norman Cousins, *Human Options: An Autobiographical Notebook* (New York: Norton, 1981), 35.

CHAPTER FIVE

Paraprofessional People Helping

IF YOU HAD A PROBLEM and needed help, to whom would you go? Think of somebody by name.

The chances are good that you chose a friend, relative, or other person who is close. In most communities there are not enough professional helpers to meet everyone's needs, and even if such help could be available, many people would avoid it.

There are several reasons for this. The professional helper is expensive, but help from a friend usually costs nothing. The professional is less available because of his or her office hours and impersonal answering service, but the peer counselor may live next door or be as near as the telephone. For some people, calling a mental-health professional may suggest a stigma that the nonprofessional does not have. "If I have to see a psychiatrist," these people reason (in most cases incorrectly), "then I really must be in bad shape!"

It is much less threatening to talk things over with a

friend in a coffee shop or to discuss problems with a neighbor. Many people appear to be afraid of professionals, view-
ing them as "mind readers" or "headshrinkers;" we rarely
think of nonprofessional people helpers in the same way.
To talk with a friend may have risks, especially if we feel
uncomfortable sharing intimate details of our life, but to
share with some stranger whom we have never met can
be much more traumatic. When I was working as a professional psychologist, a lady once came to my office and
announced that she had not slept for two nights because
of her worry about our interview together. Such anxiety
presents the professional with a rapport-building problem
that the nonprofessional almost never encounters.

If it is true that most people in need first turn to a friend
for help, then peer counseling is of great importance. In
many congregations, lay people already are doing significant
amounts of counseling and other types of caregiving in their
churches and communities. These peer helpers (sometimes
known as lay counselors or by the more technical term *para-
professionals*)[1] often recognize their limitations, but with a
little training they are able to make a significant contribution to the lives of people around them.

In our discussion of peer counseling and other forms
of nonprofessional helping, we need to look at several
important questions. Does peer counseling work? Is this
kind of helping a special gift that some people possess, or
is this something that everyone can do? If a church or other
organization wants to use paraprofessional counselors, how
are these people selected, and how should these people—
people like you—be trained? Once they are trained, what
do peer counselors actually do, and what dangers might
they encounter? These are issues that every people helper
should consider seriously.

Does Peer Counseling Work?

If you have ever had a friend help you through a crisis, you probably have concluded that peer counseling does work. But apart from our personal experiences, is there evidence that peer helping can be effective? A number of researchers have sought to answer this question, and their conclusions have been consistent. Paraprofessional or lay counselors generally are as effective as professional helpers. In a detailed book about lay counseling, Christian psychologist Siang-Yang Tan reviewed all of the research studies on the effectiveness of peer counseling. He acknowledged that there still is debate among professionals, but the overwhelming weight of evidence supports the conclusion that lay counselors frequently are as effective as professionals. There even is evidence that peer counselors often are better than professionals.[2]

One of my former professors was Dr. Joseph Matarazzo, a man who eventually became president of the American Psychological Association. After practicing psychotherapy and doing research for twenty-five years, my former teacher concluded that, except for a very small percentage of cases, like those involving people who are seriously disturbed by a severe life crisis or by immobilizing anxiety, most peer counselors are effective. What the majority of professional counselors accomplish in psychotherapy "cannot be distinguished from what is accomplished between very good friends over coffee every morning in neighborhoods and in countless work settings anywhere."[3]

Why are peer helpers effective? Several reasons have been suggested. In contrast to professionals, the peer helper is closer to the helpee, often knows him or her as a friend, and thus is better able to understand the problem, pick up nonverbal clues, and show sincere empathy. The peer helper is more often available, and because of that, he or she can provide help consistently and whenever it is needed. Often the peer counselor knows about the helpee's family, work situation, lifestyle, beliefs, or neighborhood, and this makes it easier for the helper to take a more active part in guiding decisions or helping the person in need to make life changes. In addition, lay helpers are able to communicate using words, slang, and expressions that the helpee can understand; there are no fancy psychological terms to get in the way. Finally, the lay helper is likely to be more down-to-earth, relaxed, open, informal, and inclined to introduce tension-relieving humor.

Very often the professional counselor tries to work in accordance with some highly elaborate counseling theory. He or she is concerned about using proper technique, maintaining a professional image, and succeeding as a helper. In contrast, the peer counselor usually doesn't give much thought to issues like these. He or she knows little or nothing about complex psychological theory, isn't trying to build a reputation as a counselor, and has no concerns about getting paid. Since peer counselors are concerned primarily about helping other human beings, all effort is directed toward that end. As a result, the nonprofessional often ends up doing a better job than the highly trained professional.

If all of this is true, why should any people helper bother to become a professional counselor? The answer is simpler than you might expect. While peer counselors often are effective in helping others with basic counseling problems, the more involved and complicated problems are most effectively handled by highly skilled professionals. Training is very beneficial to professional helpers, and as we will see, there is evidence that training is valuable in improving the effectiveness of peer counselors as well.

Is Counseling a Special Gift?

A bright young student once came to my office to talk about an unusual problem. He had discovered that other students kept dropping by his dormitory room to talk about their anxieties, concerns about dating, sexual struggles, fears of failure, and other problems. My student did not think he was doing anything to encourage these visits, but he was having difficulty getting his work done because of the other students who were coming for help and advice.

Periodically I hear about people like this who have no training in counseling but who discover that others keep coming for help. These people helpers have telephones that always seem to be ringing—sometimes to the consternation of their families or roommates—or people who drop by their homes or dormitory rooms at all hours of the day or night to chat about personal needs. Why do some people appear to be "natural-born" helpers, while others have no interest or seeming ability in this area at all? Might it be that some people are especially gifted or have innate abilities in the area of counseling?

Every Christian should be a people helper

According to the Bible, every Christian should have a practical and sacrificial concern for the needs of his or her fellow human beings. James reminds us repeatedly that our faith is dead if it does not show itself in a practical concern for others (James 2:14-20). This same idea is emphasized elsewhere in the Scriptures. We must all be concerned about the interests of others (Phil. 2:4). We are all instructed to rejoice with people who rejoice and to weep in supportive empathy with those who weep (Rom. 12:15). We are all told to build up one another, to admonish one another, to encourage the faint-hearted, to help the weak, and to be patient with the people around us (1 Thess. 5:11, 14). All spiritual men and women have a responsibility to gently heal or restore those who have fallen into sin, and we must all be involved in bearing one another's burdens (Gal. 6:1-2). Whenever the opportunity arises, we must "do good to all people, especially to those who belong to the family of believers" (Gal. 6:10).

Clearly, then, every Christian must reach out in love to other people, and counseling is one way in which we reach out. When family members, neighbors, fellow employees, or church members chat with us about some event in their lives or some problem issue, we who are motivated by Christian love will find ourselves counseling, whether we recognize it or not, and whether or not it is something we seek.

A special gift for some people helpers

While every Christian has a responsibility to help and counsel others, it is probable that counseling is one of the spiritual gifts that is given for building up the church and strengthening individual believers. As described in Romans 12, 1 Corinthians 12, and Ephesians 4, these gifts are more than natural abilities. They are something extra, given to believers by the Holy Spirit. Although all believers have been given one or more spiritual gifts, none of us has them all. Some Christians are especially gifted teachers, pastors, evangelists, or administrators; others are gifted as people helpers or counselors.

In Romans 12:8 we read about the gift of exhortation. The Greek word is *paraklesis,* which means "coming alongside to help." The word implies admonishing, comforting, supporting, and encouraging people to face the future. All of this sounds very much like counseling, and it all refers to a gift given by God to a select group of believers.

From this it should not be concluded that only the specially gifted are to be involved in counseling. In this respect, people helping is similar to evangelism or teaching. Although some believers have a special gift of evangelism (Eph. 4:11), every Christian is to be a witness, seeking to win men and women to

Christ. Some Christians are specially gifted as teachers (Rom. 12:7; Eph. 4:11), but all of us have the responsibility of teaching our children and others. In the same way, we must all be burden bearers and people helpers, even though some may have a special gift of counseling.

People who possess this gift are likely to have a strong desire to get involved in helping other people with their problems. They will find that their counseling efforts often bring positive and constructive results, and they will want their counseling gift to be used for building up the church. It is possible, in addition, that people with this gift are the same individuals who find themselves being approached frequently by those with counseling needs. If you wonder whether people helping is one of your spiritual gifts, ask those who know you best, and think about whether others spontaneously approach you to talk about their problems. Often other believers can see gifts that we don't see in ourselves.

Every Christian people helper, professional or paraprofessional, is the Holy Spirit's instrument to bring help and healing. It is he alone who helps people, although he often does this through us (John 14:16, 26). Undoubtedly the Holy Spirit uses all believers in this task, but those with the gift of counseling are his special agents for helping people in their times of need.

How Are Peer Counselors Selected?

The first time I ever taught a course in the basics of counseling for lay people, the church put an announcement in the bulletin, and I arrived at the appointed time expecting to meet with a few people. Instead, the room was full. There were those who were good people helpers already but who wanted to learn how to do a better job. Many in the class weren't sure that they could be helpers, but they had come to find out. Then there were a few who were steeped in their own problems and apparently had come seeking help for themselves or looking for ways to avoid their own problems by counseling others.

Probably there is some truth in the old idea that people who go into counseling often do so to solve their own problems. We might think that we *really* want to help others through our counseling, to alleviate suffering, or to make better disciples of Jesus Christ, but for all of us there may be other motives. These could include the need to feel important, to exercise power over others, to satisfy curiosity, or to have the opportunity to talk openly with our helpees about sex.

Even when we have the purest of motives, it is easy to get so emotionally involved with the problems of others that we cannot remain objective or handle the tension. The helper then begins to develop unhealthy behavior and may even urge helpees to engage in self-defeating behavior, which may then complicate the original problem. Professionals face these same dangers, but their training helps them to remain more objective and less inclined to use counseling sessions to solve their own problems; they are more willing to check their behavior and counseling motives against the objective opinion of supervisors or other counselors. The place to avoid some of these problems is right at the beginning. The prospective helper should carefully and honestly examine his or her motives for wanting to do counseling, and the teacher who gives training should do likewise.

Table 5-1 lists eight characteristics that are likely to be seen in people who are good candidates for becoming lay counselors. Some churches use psychological tests and other screening devices for selecting peer helpers,[4] but many of these are systematic ways to evaluate whether or not potential helpers have the characteristics that are summarized in the table.

| Table 5-1 | **Characteristics for Selecting People Helpers** |

From both a biblical perspective and a sound psychological perspective, the following criteria should be used to select lay Christian counselors for a lay counseling ministry:

1. *Spiritual maturity*	The counselor should be a Spirit-filled, mature Christian (cf. Gal. 6:1) who has a good knowledge of Scripture, wisdom in applying Scripture to life, and a regular prayer life.
2. *Psychological stability*	The counselor should be psychologically stable, not emotionally labile or volatile, but open and vulnerable. He or she should not be suffering from a serious psychological disorder.
3. *Love for and interest in people*	The counselor should be a warm, caring, and genuine person with a real interest in people and their welfare.
4. *Spiritual gifts*	The counselor should possess appropriate spiritual gifts, such as exhortation (other examples may include wisdom, knowledge, discerning of spirits, mercy, and healing).
5. *Life experience*	The counselor should have had some life experience and hence not be too young.
6. *Previous training or experience in helping people*	Often experience can be helpful, although it is not an absolute necessity for effective helping.
7. *Ability to maintain confidentiality*	The counselor should be able to maintain confidentiality and protect the privacy of clients.
8. *Diversity*	In selecting a variety of counselors, it is helpful to have people who represent both sexes and differences in age, education, socioeconomic status, and ethnic/cultural background.

Adapted from Siang-Yang Tan, Lay Counseling: Equipping Christians for a Helping Ministry (Grand Rapids: Zondervan, 1991), 100, 102.

How Are Peer Counselors Trained?

At one time in his career, Dr. Paul Tournier wondered if he should become a psychiatrist, but his friends in psychiatry discouraged this. "Don't become one of us," they warned. "Such training could stifle you and take away your warmth and spontaneity."

For nonprofessionals, the problem is not so much whether a peer counselor should get training. The real issue concerns the *kind* of training that one gets. Professional training programs frequently focus on sophisticated research methods, complex personality theories, and complicated analyses of case histories. All of this pulls the trainee away from people and teaches him or her that knowledge of techniques or conformity to some counseling theory is of greater importance than rubbing elbows with people who are hurting.

In contrast, the nonprofessional is often less psychological than the professional, less concerned about making the right diagnosis or using the best technique, and not at all interested in theory or research. This person wants to help others but often is unwilling to sit through a long, complicated training program. The training that he or she gets, therefore, is usually brief but intensely practical and geared toward developing empathy, warmth, genuineness, and the other traits that lead to effective counseling. Training for peer counselors (and probably for professionals) should be down-to-earth and practical, dealing with the real problems that real people have in their lives. While professionals can contribute a great deal to the training process, we also can learn from other peer counselors and even from our helpees.

A number of different programs have been developed for training peer counselors, but some aspects of this training are common to almost all of the approaches. The following paragraphs can be helpful in training you to be a better helper, and they give guidelines that might be used for training others.

Focus on the person

Effective training will *focus on the prospective counselor as a person.* If "in any helping relationship, the personality, values, attitudes and beliefs of the helper are of primary importance," then these should be of primary importance in a training program. The helper's strong and weak points should be considered. If you want to help people by counseling, you should examine yourself in the light of Scripture (Ps. 119:9-11; 139:23-24) and seek with God's help to make appropriate changes in your life. You should look at your special abilities and gifts, and you should be honest enough to talk about yourself to one or two others. A good way to know yourself better is to disclose yourself to God and to fellow human beings whom you trust (James 5:16).

As the peer counselor begins his or her work, there will often be a need for encouragement and psychological support, especially when the counseling gets difficult. The beginner (and the "pro" as well) may feel a need to discuss his or her insecurities as a helper, or there might be a need to talk about the anxieties and temptations that can come when we are closely involved with the intimate details of another person's life. Beginning counselors should find a way to talk over these issues with someone who is a more experienced helper.

Learn skills

One of the most widely used textbooks for training counselors is *The Skilled Helper.*[5] The author, a professor at Loyola University of Chicago, has written an entire training program to teach what he calls "helping skills." Counseling theory and knowledge about human problems can be important for people helpers, but ultimately the best helper is the man or woman who possesses the skills that make it easier to accurately understand and positively influence the helpee.

Effective training for helpers involves the teaching and learning of skills. This involves learning what needs to be done, watching others as they demonstrate skills, and then practicing the skills. These are three steps that we follow when we learn to play golf or to make music on the piano. Knowing, watching, and doing are important in the learning of all skills, including the skill of people helping.

Provide experience
Effective training must include on-the-job experience. A statement like this can make professional counselors feel uncomfortable. It seems to suggest that novice people helpers should be turned loose to learn by "playing psychiatrist," trying to help unsuspecting troubled people solve their problems. We should remember, however, that lay people already are counseling real people, so our task is to help them do better what they already are doing.

The idea that long periods of training must come before practice, is crumbling in many professional training programs. Medical students and nurses, for example, go on the wards very early in their training. We get new converts involved in witnessing soon after their conversion. The same kind of on-the-job training, accompanied by supervision from more experienced people, is likely to characterize future peer counselor training as well.

What Are Some Dangers of Peer Counseling?
Several years ago a young man on the West Coast committed suicide. Following the funeral, his parents sued a large evangelical church, charging that members of the pastoral staff had given incompetent counseling. As a result, according

to the suit, the man was prevented from getting the help that might have saved his life. The lawsuit eventually was dismissed, and experts who examined the records concluded that the church counselors had done nothing wrong, unethical, or incompetent. But the publicity surrounding the case alerted a lot of churches to a reality that nobody thought about a few years ago. In the United States, unlike most other parts of the world, lawsuits are very common; all counselors, including pastors and lay people helpers, can be sued by disgruntled helpees or their families.

Lay helpers might also be surprised to find that in some places their activities violate the law. If you accept money for doing counseling, for example, you are officially practicing a profession without a license, and this is illegal. If you call yourself a psychologist or counselor, but you don't have professional certification, this also can be a violation of the law. For this reason, many Christians avoid the word *counseling* and, instead, use the terms *lay helper, lay minister,* or *people helper.* In every promotion of what we do, great care must be taken to avoid misleading claims about our expertise, competence, or abilities to bring change.[6]

None of this is meant to scare you away from giving help. Instead, it is a warning to be careful in how you represent your expertise. If you work within a church setting, the church leaders should be cautious as well and consider getting legal guidance before starting a peer counseling ministry.

Legal issues are not the only potential dangers in people helping. Sometimes we can get so involved with the problems of others that our own stability or family relationships suffer. At times, all helpers face burnout because they are so involved in caregiving that they fail to rest and to take time for their own needs. On occasion you might "get in over your head" and discover that somebody is threatening suicide or harm to others—perhaps to you—and you aren't sure where to turn for immediate help. For peer counselors, however, four other issues lurk with special prominence. If you are aware of these, you are much better able to avoid the dangers.

Counselor curiosity

In everyday conversation we avoid talking about some issues because they are too personal. We rarely ask other people about their finances, their sex life, their anxieties, or the status of their marriage. In a helping relationship, however, these topics are often discussed openly because they may be the very issues that are bothering the person who needs help.

This freedom to talk openly can raise some ethical issues that the peer helper would be wise to heed. First is the issue of *counselor curiosity.* Sometimes in our counseling we temporarily forget the helpee's needs and start asking for information that primarily satisfies our own curiosity. The helper must be alert to this tendency and seek to avoid it, especially when the topic of conversation deals with issues that border on gossip or on the details of the helpee's sexual behavior.

Sexual stimulation

Closely connected with this is the issue of *sexual stimulation.* This can go both ways: The helper can be stimulated by an attractive helpee, or the person who wants help might be attracted to the helper. We may stimulate the other person or be stimulated without intending or expecting this, without either of us being aware of what is happening. The male helper who puts his arm around the helpee to give comfort may not realize that his female or male helpee might misinterpret the meaning of the hug. A modest amount of physical contact between helper and helpee is not necessarily wrong, since at times this can be very supportive and encouraging. But we must be careful to ask, How does the helpee interpret this? and What satisfaction is this contact giving me?

It is absolutely crucial that the Christian helper avoid all appearance of evil. By forgetting this principle, some counselors—including pastoral counselors—have become overly involved with their helpees and as a result have ruined their families, lives, reputations, and ministries. To say, "This would never happen to me," is to already be walking on dangerous ground (1 Cor. 10:12).

Confidence leaks

Confidence leaks are a third danger for the peer helper. It is true that the peer helper is not legally bound by the same confidentiality code that is so important to professionals. But a peer counselor talking about his or her helpees borders on gossip and can do a lot of harm. Even when we try to hide the details of a case, it is possible that somebody in the neighborhood or church will guess who is being talked about. Such talk should be avoided. It does nothing for our spiritual well-being and may very well shake the helpee's faith in the helper.

Spiritual balance

Underemphasis or overemphasis on the spiritual can be another danger. In the case of underemphasis, the helpee is denied the resources of the Scriptures or prayer and sometimes never even hears the gospel because the helper is afraid to raise the issue. In contrast, when there is an overemphasis on religion, the helpee might be driven away—scared off by religion—or be led to believe that the spiritual part of our being is all that matters. Such a view has no support in Scripture, nor can we maintain the view that all problems will vanish automatically if we are right with the Lord. The spiritual must enter our counseling, since it is crucially important, but it should be in balance with other issues, rather than under- or over-emphasized.

Avoiding the dangers

How can we avoid these and other dangers? For one thing, we can develop spiritual protection. Daily study of the Scriptures and consistent prayer, even during the counseling session, can keep our minds from wandering and our mouths from saying something harmful or even sinful. Second, it helps when we are alert to the dangers. To be forewarned is to be forearmed! Third, we can deliberately seek to avoid compromising situations, overemphasis on sexually arousing topics, and other dangers. Finally, we can get into the habit of discussing our counseling *in confidence* with some other person—a pastor, a professional counselor, or simply a friend who can help us keep things in perspective and free from danger.

The worst danger of all

The training and use of peer counselors to help others is an exciting concept that has become widely accepted in the church. We train church people to witness. We teach them how to teach others, and now we are training them how to disciple others. Surely as a part of this we should be training them how to *relate to* others—to bear one another's burdens and to counsel with each other.

There are dangers in people helping, but there can also be tremendous benefits, especially when the peer counselors have had some practical training. It is true, of course, that a little knowledge about counseling can be a dangerous thing, but no knowledge and training can be even worse. And to have no concern about helping others on a peer-to-peer level may be the worst danger of all.

Notes

1. In this chapter, I am using the terms *peer counseling* and *paraprofessional* counseling interchangeably. Technically, they mean something different. Peer counselors are people helpers who have little or no training in counseling skills. Paraprofessional counselors— like paramedics or paralegals—often have a lot of training in counseling methods, even though they lack professional credentials.
2. For a summary of the research on lay counseling effectiveness, see Siang-Yang Tan, *Lay Counseling: Equipping Christians for a Helping Ministry* (Grand Rapids: Zondervan, 1991), 62–65.
3. J. Matarazzo, "Comment on Licensing," *A. P. A. Monitor* 10 (September-October 1979): 36.
4. For a description of these tools, see Tan's book, pages 96–110.
5. Gerard Egan, *The Skilled Helper,* fourth ed. (Monterey, Calif.: Brooks/Cole, 1994).
6. For an excellent treatment of legal issues relating to counseling see George Ohlschlager and Peter Mosgofian, *Law for the Christian Counselor* (Dallas: Word, 1992).

CHAPTER SIX

Stress and People Helping

WHAT WOULD LIFE BE like if we didn't have any stress? If you are like most people in this stress-saturated society, you might answer that life without stress would be a lot simpler. It also would be a lot duller, a lot less challenging, and maybe even a lot shorter. Some researchers have argued that we need at least some stress to keep us alive and moving—that the only people without stress are dead people. But the same researchers know that too much stress can kill us.

According to Hans Selye, a Canadian scientist who devoted his life to the study of this topic, stress can be divided into two categories. *Distress* is the type of stress that is unpleasant and harmful. Grief, the experience of failure, immobilizing anxiety, depression, and physical illness are all examples. In contrast, *eustress* is a positive experience. Getting a promotion, moving to a new house, attending a wedding, or winning a game can all put the body under stress, but it is a pleasant type of stress. Some people like the stress of a fast-paced life or a challenging job because it is motivating and invigorating. The two types of stress put our bodies under pressure and force us to cope, but eustress is much more pleasant and more fun than the painful experiences of distress.

People helpers are in the business of dealing with stress in other people and in themselves. Not many people talk to a counselor about eustress, but almost all helpees come for help because they are distressed. We can be better people helpers if we understand what stress is, know how it affects us, and are able to help people cope better with the stresses that are part of everybody's life.

What Is Stress?

"Do you want me to ruin your day now or later?"

Several years ago I wrote a book about stress. I dug into psychological books and research articles, talked to people about their stresses, wrote about coping with stress, and then realized that I was under a lot of stress myself. I was reminded of this when I typed the words *What Is Stress?* at the beginning of this section and was interrupted by my administrative assistant, who asked when I wanted to have my day ruined. The problem concerned a business issue that should have been handled earlier but slipped through the cracks. It really was a minor problem, but it came as a very fresh reminder that stress—the distress kind—can raise an ugly fist at any time, can influence us emotionally, can interfere with our efficiency, and can ruin some of our days.

It is difficult to give a definition of stress that everybody will accept. Often we talk about stress in terms of the circumstances of life. We may say, for example, that we have stress at work, financial stress, or the stress of living in a home where there is a lot of conflict. It is more accurate, however, and probably less confusing, to think of stress as something that happens inside the person. Stress is a physiological and psychological response to the demands of life. Selye originally defined stress as the wear and tear of living. Stress for one person may differ from that experienced by somebody else, but every day each of us experiences physical and emotional wear and tear that results from the pressures of life.

Table 6-1 might enable us to understand the meaning of stress more clearly and could be useful when we try to help others. The diagram suggests that stress has four components: sources, perception, effects, and symptoms. There can be many *sources* of stress, including the influence of past experiences and the impact of present events or circumstances—like the "day-ruining" news that came from my assistant. The source of stress often is out in the workplace, the neighbor-

Table 6-1 **The Sources, Perception, Effects, and Symptoms of Stress**

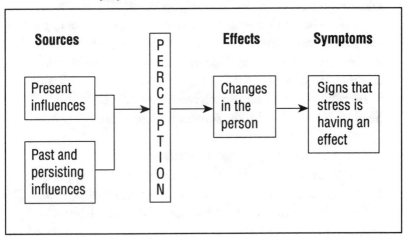

95

hood, the home, or elsewhere in the environment. But sometimes stress has its source in the brain. People who worry a lot, for example, create stress for themselves.

Perception, the second part of the diagram, refers to how we view the stress-inducing events. What might seem bad or potentially bad in the minds of some people might not be viewed in the same way by others. If the basketball team in my hometown wins a championship, the final score is the same, but the people in our neighborhood perceive this as good news and experience enthusiastic eustress. The losers see the situation differently, and some are under a lot of distress.

There also are differences in the *effects* of stress. The same stressful situation can influence people in a variety of ways. This can lead to differences in the ways that we show our stresses. If a person comes to you for help, you might not be aware of the sources of stress in that person's life, you may not know how he or she is perceiving a life situation, and you might be in the dark about how the individual is being influenced by the stress. But often we can see some of the *symptoms* of stress.

People who go to counselors often complain first about their discomforts and symptoms. To help them, the place to start is often at the right of the diagram. We look at the symptoms and then move from right to left, trying to lessen the effects of stress by helping people perceive events differently and by helping them cope with the sources of their distress.

The Sources and Perception of Stress

We don't have to be experts in stress management to know that stress can come from a variety of sources, some of which occur in the present while others arise from the past.

Present influences

As Table 6-2 shows, the present stresses are of four types. Physical stresses include infections and disease, the influence of drugs, the effects of diet, or even the stress that comes when we don't get enough sleep. We all know that illness can put us under stress, but so can fatigue, too much coffee or sugar, a lack of exercise, or a toothache.

Psychological stress most often comes in the form of

Table 6-2 **Some Present Stressful Influences**

Physical (Biological) Stresses	Psychological Stresses

1. Infection and/or disease
2. Brain damage
3. Drugs
4. Biological deprivation
  • Sleep deprivation
  • Lack of balanced diet
  • Lack of exercise
  • Lack of oxygen, etc.
	1. Frustration, including bore-dom
	2. Conflict
	3. Internal anxieties, conflicts, or insecurities
	4. External pressure
	5. Self-generated pressure
	6. Fear of circumstances, closeness, failure, and other anxieties
	7. Too much or too rapid change

Social (Sociological) Stresses	Spiritual Stresses
1. Marital conflict 2. Occupational and economic tensions 3. Pressure from other people 4. Civilian catastrophe 5. War and other national events 6. Accidents 7. Technological change	1. Conviction of sin 2. Guilt 3. Spiritual drifting 4. Dissension within the church 5. Direct satanic influence

frustrations, conflicts with other people, internal anxieties and insecurities, or pressures. A demanding boss or a whining child can put us under pressure, but so can our own self-expectations. Most of us have discovered that some of our greatest pressures come from insecurities and the expectations or demands that we put on ourselves.

Social stress, the third of the four types, comes from the societies where we live or the people with whom we interact. These are the stresses that come from our marriages, bosses, professors, policemen who stop us for speeding, and—every April—from unknown people in the tax department.

Finally, spiritual stress comes from a conviction that we have sinned, from a failure to worship or to maintain a closeness to Christ, and often from tensions within the church. Christians are in a spiritual battle (Eph. 6:12-13). We recognize that the devil and his forces can drag us down spiritually but can also create increased stress in the physical, psychological, and social parts of our life.

Past and persisting influences

How a person responds to stress in the present often depends on the experiences that he or she had in the past. While browsing in a bookstore one day, I came across a book by Susan Forward entitled *Toxic Parents: Overcoming Their Hurtful Legacy and Reclaiming Your Life* (New York: Bantam Books, 1989). A few months later this was followed by *Toxic Faith: Understanding and Overcoming Religious Addiction* by Stephen Arterburn and Jack Felton (Nashville: Oliver-Nelson Books, 1991) and by other books that point to the present-day impact of harmful past influences in our lives. Often these past influences continue to persist and make us more susceptible to the current stresses of life.

Once again, we can divide these influences into four categories as shown in Table 6-3. These are influences from the past that determine, in part, how we will respond to present stress. The physical past and persisting influences include the effects of heredity, prior disease, or previous addiction to drugs. Psychological past and persisting influences might include the fact

Table 6-3 **Some Past and Persisting Influences**

Physical (Biological) Influences	Psychological Influences

1. Inherited characteristics
2. Congenital and acquired defects
3. Prior or chronic disease
4. Drug addiction
5. Other persisting physical conditions
	1. Early upbringing
	  • Parental deprivation, neglect, or abuse
	  • Rejection or overprotection
	  • Parental overprotection, overindulgence, or over-permissiveness
	  • Rigid, perfectionistic demands
	2. Family disharmony/dysfunctional families
	3. Early trauma
	4. Inadequate learning experiences

Social (Sociological) Influences	Spiritual Influences
1. Race or other minority group membership 2. Socioeconomic status 3. Educational level 4. Place of residence 5. Religious affiliation 6. Marital status 7. Sex (and sexual orientation) 8. Place of residence	1. Feelings of spiritual worthlessness or failure 2. Ongoing spiritual emptiness 3. Lack of faith in Christ 4. Involvement in a rigid religious group or other "toxic faith" religious group 5. Misconceptions about Christianity

that we grew up in "toxic" or dysfunctional families, experienced a previous trauma that has left us psychologically
wounded, or were deprived of the opportunity to learn effective social skills. Social past and persisting influences could
include the ways we have been shaped by race, socioeconomic
level, educational backgrounds, or affiliation with a religious
group. Fourth, spiritual past and persisting influences could
involve a recurring sense that "I will never be able to please
God," an ongoing spiritual emptiness, or a sense of frustration
because we can't meet the demands of a religious leader.

Since we all experience different stresses and we all have
different backgrounds, it follows that none of us experiences
stress in the same way. And the problem is made more complex by our differences in perception.

Seeing things differently

When my elderly mother lived in a retirement home, she ate
her meals with three other residents. These four ladies sat
around the same table three times every day and were living
in very similar circumstances, but apparently they all had
different views about the food, the place where they lived,
and the people who worked there. Differences like these are
not limited to older people. Each of us brings a unique perspective to the events and stresses of life. When students are
facing the same final exam, some react calmly while others
are highly anxious. People who experience natural disasters,
such as floods or tornadoes, all encounter similar danger, but
they view their stresses differently.

What accounts for these differences? Personality variations
probably have an influence, and so does our record of past
experience in coping. People who have coped effectively with
stress in the past are more likely to see a new stress as one more
challenge, unlike those who may not have coped well earlier.

The issues of threat and control also influence how we will perceive a stressful situation. When a situation is seen as threatening, it is highly stressful, especially for people who don't believe that they have the resources or abilities to cope. Our views of stress also depend, in part, on whether or not we feel in control of a situation. Many years ago, for example, it was found that surgery patients perceive their operations as being less stressful and recover more quickly when they are given realistic expectations beforehand and are aware of some things they can do to take control of the recovery process. Christians who know that God ultimately is in control are inclined to view the difficulties of life differently than those who are nonbelievers.

When we understand the nature of our stresses and have an idea of how long they will last, we handle the situation better when the stresses do come. To understand how people are influenced by stress, therefore, we should try to determine how they perceive their circumstances and their own abilities to cope.

The Impact of Stress

Stress not only is perceived in different ways, it also influences us in different ways. Several years ago, cardiologists in San Francisco suggested that people can be divided into two broad categories, Type A and Type B. Nobody fits the categories exactly, but according to the doctors, Type A people are highly ambitious, aggressive, competitive, self-driving, and pushing to be successful. Much different are Type B people who are more casual, relaxed, and less concerned about achievement. After years of study, the physicians who proposed these two categories reported that people who live a Type A lifestyle are seven times more likely to have a heart attack than those with a Type B way of living.

In the high-pressure society where we live, most of us know that stressful Type A living can have a powerful, sometimes life-threatening, influence on our bodies. Something similar happens when we work in a demanding job, live under continual threat or danger, aren't able to control our lives or circumstances, and in other ways go through weeks or years of constant strain. We wear down physically and psychologically. Our relationships with others deteriorate, and we often feel cut off from God. In the midst of such circumstances it is easy to develop sour, bitter, or hopeless attitudes, and these, in turn, create more stress.

Outsiders don't always see these changes, but they wear away at our bodies and in time show themselves in signs or symptoms. When these symptoms persist or get too hard to live with, we often go to doctors, counselors, or friends who can give help.

The Signs and Symptoms of Stress

How do you respond when you are under stress? Probably most of us have our own ways of reacting to the pressures of life, and the ways in which you respond may be different from the ways your friends or family respond. Table 6-4 (the final chart in this chapter—I promise) lists some of the more common reactions to stress. Of course, only medically trained people are qualified to diagnose and treat the physical symptoms that arise from and sometimes create stress. In a similar way, professional counselors are best equipped to use carefully designed psychological tests and similar methods to better understand the psychological symptoms that accompany stress.

By observing others and listening as they talk, all of us can get some indication of how stress is affecting our helpees. When I am under stress, for example, I tend to withdraw and to get negative and impatient. My family does not need a sophisticated medical or psychological examination to know what is going on. We can learn a lot

Table 6-4 **Some Signs and Symptoms of Stress**

Physical Symptoms	**Psychological Symptoms**
1. Changes in blood pressure and the flow of blood 2. Increased blood glucose concentration 3. Gastrointestinal changes, sometimes leading to ulcers 4. Reduced ability to resist illness, increases in stress-triggered diseases 5. Changes in muscle strength, including back problems 6. Increase in cardiovascular disease	1. An increased tendency to attack or to withdraw (fight or flight) 2. Use of defense mechanisms 3. Psychological behavior such as • misperceptions • excessive worry • distorted thinking (making invalid assumptions or reaching wrong conclusions) • inappropriate emotional expression • repetitious physical activity (such as pacing or biting nails) • inappropriate or unusual ways of relating to others • disorientation and confusion • other odd behavior
Social (Sociological) Symptoms	**Spiritual Symptoms**
1. Breakdown in the way people relate (for example, families fall apart, churches split into factions, fellow employees undercut one another) 2. Social movements, such as strikes, riots, revolutions, or wars	1. Prolonged feelings of guilt, doubt, spiritual failure, or self-condemnation 2. A sense of being cut off from God 3. Continual spiritual searching 4. Fanaticism and/or involvement in cults

by keeping our eyes and ears open and by seeking to be sensitive to what another person's words and behavior really communicate.

Helping People Handle Stress

Jeff Alm was a football player with a bright future. He distinguished himself on the Notre Dame team and later was drafted by the Houston Oilers. Described by his agent as "an unusual guy" who was intelligent, unassuming, and inclined to laugh a lot, Jeff Alm was driving a car one night when he lost control on a freeway overpass, and his best friend was catapulted out of the vehicle and onto the pavement twenty-five feet below, where he died. In the confusion of that accident scene, the young football player reached into his car for a gun, stuck it in his mouth, and pulled the trigger. In different ways, Jeff Alm's friends and a host of newspaper reporters tried to make sense of the tragedy, but they agreed that he had taken his life in a moment of shock, overwhelming stress, and probable guilt over his friend's death.

This is a tragic and extreme example of how one man responded to intense stress. In a similar situation, you or I might have responded in very different ways—some of which could have been almost as destructive as Jeff Alm's suicide. Every counselor knows that intense stress throws some people into deep depression or other mental illness, excessive use of alcohol and other drugs, or stress-induced physical sickness and deterioration. Severe stress often lowers a person's efficiency or ability to concentrate, leads to exhaustion, makes it more difficult to cope with additional pressures, disrupts relationships, and lowers the body's ability to fight disease.

But there are healthier ways to cope ourselves and to help other people deal with stress. First, there is value in *taking inventory* of the situation. This can have a calming effect and help put stressful situations in perspective. Sometimes we can do this ourselves with a notebook, but often it helps if we can talk with a caring helper. Ask, for example, what really is causing the stress. Are we seeing the situation accurately? What might be done to tackle the problem? What has been found to work in similar situations? When there are several stresses, one almost always takes priority over the others. It is best to work on the stress that is most disturbing or most disruptive and to move on to the others later. Sometimes the place to start is with the recognition that some things might be forever different because of the stressful situation that is now being faced.

Stress often forces us to adjust; that is what makes it so difficult at times. But *making changes* can also be a healthy response to stress. We can change—or help others change—our environments, perceptions, bodies, and skills. To change the environment, consider eliminating some things from your schedule, changing jobs, moving away from friendships with people who create stress in you, or finding some time to reflect. To change perceptions, recognize that we often lose perspective in times of difficulty. Some events, like dangerous weather conditions or a terminal illness, cannot be changed, but even then we can change the way we view things. Alone, or with the help of another person, try to get a more balanced view of what has happened and how we are responding.

Sometimes we forget that stress can be handled better when we pay attention to our bodies. Simple things like getting sufficient rest, eating balanced meals, or taking time for exercise, can enable us to rise more effectively to the pressures of modern living.

Then we can change our skills. Suppose a person is facing

the stresses of being unemployed. Perhaps that person needs help in writing a resume, handling interviews better, or getting additional training in some trade or profession. To change what we know and what we can do is a way to change the impact of stress.

In addition to taking inventory and making changes, *anticipating future stress* can also help, especially if the anticipation comes before the stress. In the research that was mentioned earlier, surgery patients who had a realistic indication of what was coming were better able to handle their preoperative and postoperative stress, and after the surgery their physical conditions improved faster.[1] This has been called *stress inoculation.* It is a process of helping people understand what is ahead so that they are less surprised, more knowledgeable, and less inclined to be immobilized by fear and uncertainty when the anticipated stress comes.

In addition, Christians handle stress better when we are *drawing on our spiritual resources.* Never underestimate the power of prayer, the comfort that comes from reading and reflecting on Scripture, the lift that comes from corporate worship, the value of reminding ourselves about the nature of God, or the support that comes from fellow believers.

This brings us to one more healthy means for coping: *finding social support.* If some caring person had been at the side of Jeff Alm when he reached for the gun, he probably would be alive today. Researchers have confirmed what most of us know already: The presence and support of other people significantly moderates the effects of stress and makes coping more effective. In contrast, when people lack support from others and from their environments, stresses have a more potent impact, and the person's ability to cope is lessened.[2]

The people helper can assist others in taking inventory, making changes, sometimes anticipating stress, and drawing

on the strength and comfort that comes from God. Often
people find that the presence of a caring individual is a great
help in times of stress, especially if that caregiver is a believer
in the God of all comfort. At times, our very presence is a
source of encouragement.

Giving Encouragement

The Bible instructs us to encourage one another, and at
times we all need to be encouraged by others (Rom. 1:11-12;
1 Thess. 4:18; 5:11; Heb. 3:13; 10:24-25). One of the most
admired individuals in the New Testament was a man from
Cyprus named Joseph. He was so inclined to encourage
others that the early church members changed his name and
called him Barnabas, which means "son of encouragement."
Several times he makes an appearance in Scripture, usually
doing something that encourages others.[3]

Shortly after Paul became a Christian, for example, many of
the believers weren't sure he could be trusted. They had reason
to be suspicious since Paul had been the chief persecutor of the
church. But Barnabas encouraged Paul, brought him to the
apostles, and stood by him when others were still wary.

Many years later, in what probably was the last of his
epistles, Paul showed that he too had learned how to be
an encourager. (Perhaps he had learned from Barnabas.)
The old apostle was in a cold damp prison when he put
his words on the parchment. There was no complaining.
Instead, Paul wrote a positive letter of encouragement to
Timothy, the younger man who would take over after his
mentor was gone. The letter begins with thanks to God,
even in the midst of difficult circumstances (2 Tim. 1:3).

Then Paul wrote about *prayer.* Sometimes when people
need encouragement and help, prayer is all we can give. In
reality, it is the best we can give. Can you imagine how

encouraged Timothy must have felt to read that he constantly was being remembered in prayer by the saintly apostle Paul (v. 3)?

Paul also encouraged Timothy by helping him *keep things in perspective*. The letter mentioned the tears that had come when the two men parted, commented about Timothy's upbringing, reminded him of his calling to the ministry, and emphasized that although God allows suffering he still is all powerful (vv. 4-8).

Throughout the letter, Paul continues *giving guidance* and advice to his younger colleague. Guard what was given to you, Paul wrote. Train younger men to do what you do. Do your best to be a good workman. Flee from evil, quarreling, and greed. Strive, instead, to be holy.

As he read, Timothy must have been encouraged by the guidance of his older friend, but he also may have been challenged because Paul *encouraged action*. "Do your best to come to me quickly," he wrote. "When you come, bring the cloak that I left . . . and my scrolls" (2 Tim. 4:9, 13). He charged Timothy to preach: correcting, rebuking, and encouraging others with patience and careful instruction (v. 2). There are times when spurring people to action is an effective way to give them encouragement.

If you want to be a people helper and you don't know where to start, you can become an encourager—starting right now. Pray for those who need encouragement. Send a card or a note to someone who might not expect it—a relative, a secretary, a pastor or other Christian leader, a former teacher. Look for an opportunity to encourage somebody every day by giving a compliment, saying thanks, expressing your appreciation for what someone has done or is doing. Like Paul in prison, you might find that encouraging others helps dull some of the pain and struggles that might be in your own life. Sometimes it is surprising how much a kind word of encouragement can cheer up another person (Prov. 12:25; 25:11) and encourage the encourager.

A California college professor recently was watching television when he heard that "another random act of senseless violence" had occurred in his community. As he watched the newscaster, the professor wondered what it would be like to have a community where people showed random acts of senseless *kindness.*

The next day, he gave his students an unusual assignment: to do something out of the ordinary to help somebody. They were to write about their experiences. The students responded with enthusiasm. One young man bought twenty blankets at the Salvation Army store and gave them to homeless people under a bridge. Another waved a motorist into a nearby parking space and drove to the only other available space almost half a mile away.

Somebody in a local bank heard about the experiment and printed bumper stickers urging people to "commit a random act of senseless kindness." The stickers were sold for a dollar each, and the money was given to a local charity. The police department put the stickers on their cars. The idea was broadcast from radio stations, spread in schools, and encouraged from pulpits.

The professor was stunned and excited. It seemed that almost everybody in the community of one hundred thousand people wanted to get involved. For a time, at least, the people were applying a basic biblical principle of encouragement: Be ye kind, one to another.

And it had an impact on the whole city.

Notes
1. Irving L. Janis, *Psychological Stress: Psychological and Behavioral Studies of Surgical Patients* (New York: Wiley, 1958).

2. Robert C. Carson and James Butcher, *Abnormal Psychology and Modern Life* (New York: HarperCollins, 1992), 144.

3. Within the past several years, encouragement has become a popular subject among Christians, and several books have appeared to emphasize its importance. Among these are *Encouraging One Another* by Gene A. Getz (Wheaton: Victor Books, 1982) and *Encouragement: Key to Caring* by Lawrence Crabb and Dan B. Allender (Grand Rapids: Zondervan, 1984). One British writer has called encouragement "the Barnabas factor." See Derek Wood, *The Barnabas Factor: The Power of Encouragement* (Leicester, England: Inter-Varsity Press, 1988).

CHAPTER SEVEN

Helping in a Crisis

AS WE GO THROUGH LIFE, all of us encounter
crises at least occasionally. The death of someone we love, the
birth of a deformed child, the breakdown of a marriage, the
failure to be accepted into college, involvement in a car accident—all are events that shake us and leave us feeling threatened, anxious, confused, and often depressed. Stated somewhat
formally, *a crisis is any event or series of circumstances that threat-
ens a person's well-being and interferes with his or her routines of
daily living.* Crises are stressful because they disrupt our lives,
often have long-lasting implications, and force us to find ways
of coping that we may not have tried before.

Most of us move along from day to day, meeting the problems and challenges of life in a more or less efficient manner.
Periodically, however, a situation arises that is so novel and
threatening that our usual ways of handling problems no
longer work. Suddenly we are forced to rely on new and
untried methods to deal with the pressures and tension.

In the past, people first turned to relatives in times of crises, seeking their advice and accepting their help, guidance, and sympathy. In many parts of the world, this still happens, but in much of North America things are different. We are a mobile people who move frequently and often are far away from family members who could give the greatest support in times of crisis. In the absence of relatives we turn to neighbors, friends, coworkers, fellow church members, and pastors. Often these people appear on the scene in times of crises, and often they are very helpful.

Crises Are Not All the Same
Crises can be divided into two broad categories. *Developmental crises* occur at predicted times as we journey through life. Facing the first day in school, coping with adolescence, adjusting to marriage, dealing with the insecurities of middle age, adapting to retirement—all are crisis situations that require extra effort on the part of individuals and their families. These crises may be very severe, but usually they can be predicted in advance and are resolved as the individual learns to adjust to the new stage in life.

Accidental crises, as the name implies, are much less predictable, and as a result they often hit with greater force. Being laid off from work without warning, learning that a friend has died in a traffic accident, or having an engagement end unexpectedly, are examples of situations that put extreme demands on the people involved and often leave us confused about what to do next.

How we react to crises
In times of crisis, most people turn to their habitual ways of dealing with problems. Very soon, however, it becomes clear that the old coping devices aren't working. The initial stress is still there, but the person in crisis also feels frustration

and confusion because of the inability to cope. At this point all of one's inner resources are mobilized. The person tries a number of trial-and-error methods to deal with the problem, attempts to think of creative new ways for dealing with the situation, and strives to accept or to make the best of circumstances that cannot be changed. If all of this fails and the problem continues, the individual eventually collapses physically, mentally, or both. Often this is what happens in a so-called nervous breakdown. There are no more resources or stamina left for coping with the stress. So the person gives up, exhausted. Sometimes he or she withdraws into a world of unreality or persists irrationally in behavior that may hide or deny the problem but does nothing to solve it.

The uniqueness of crises

Every crisis situation is unique. What happens in times of crisis will depend in part on the circumstances, personalities, and psychological makeup of the people involved; the availability of others who can help; one's past experience (or lack of it) in handling crises; and the severity of the stress. When stress is intense, some people almost immediately collapse psychologically and physically. Others discover that they have tremendous inner reserves that enable them to cope with even prolonged periods of intense pressure.

Some characteristics, however, are seen in nearly everybody during times of crisis. *Anxiety*, for example, is almost always present. In some cases this can be so intense that it interferes with clear thinking and causes people to act inappropriately or to make poor decisions that, in turn, add to the original problems. Often there is a sense of *helplessness*. The person doesn't know what to do and frequently feels ashamed because he or she cannot be more self-reliant. A *dependence on others* almost is inevitable, but this, too, can create problems. Sometimes the person feels guilty for being so dependent, frustrated with the inability to make decisions, and angry because other people are running his or her life. All of this can contribute to a *loss of self-esteem* because the person feels vulnerable and not in control. *Anger* over the whole situation is a common emotion that sometimes is hidden but often directed at others—including the people who are trying to help. In the midst of frustration, the person in a crisis doesn't know who to be angry at, so he or she lashes out against those who are closest and most likely to remain faithful and supportive despite the outbursts of anger. Sometimes there is anger at God, followed by feelings of guilt. And there may be *decreasing efficiency* in one's daily behavior: ruminating on the problem, worrying about what will happen next, questioning why it happened in the first place. All of these characteristics draw away the time, energy, and attention that normally would be directed to other activities.

Helping People Cope with Crises

A crisis is more than an increase in tension or a disruption of our schedules. Crises often turn our life in different directions, and the ways in which we respond can have a bearing on our future adjustment and mental health.

If we are able to cope with the crisis, to adapt to our new circumstances, or to find efficient ways for solving the crisis problem, then we develop greater self-confidence and experience. This, in turn, will enable us to deal more effectively with future crises. On the other hand, if a person is unable to cope, there are feelings of failure or incompetence that spill over to the next crisis and make it even harder to adapt in the future.

In times of crises most of us try to mobilize our own inner resources, and sometimes we seek the assistance of professional counselors. Often, however, the best helpers are those who the person in crisis already knows, respects, and loves. The closer you are to the person in crisis and the more you are aware of the situation, the more likely you are to be called on and the easier it may be for you to intervene on your own initiative.

How can we help a person in a time of crisis? To begin, we might examine Table 7-1. This shows some unhealthy and healthy ways of dealing with a crisis. When sickness, death in the family, financial losses, marital strife, and other crises come along, the counselor's goal is to help the person avoid unhealthy behaviors, feelings, or thoughts and to focus instead on what is healthy and constructive.

To do this most effectively, the helper must be geographically near the person in crisis (it is difficult—although not impossible—to help someone from a distance), immediately available (even if this means in the middle of the night), mobile (so that the helper can go to the person in need, if necessary), and flexible in helping methods. The people who can best meet these criteria are family members, friends, neighbors, church members, and ministers. The latter can be especially helpful in times of crisis because they symbolize hope and theological stability to a person in the midst of discouragement and great uncertainty.

As you read about *crisis intervention* in the following paragraphs, you will notice that the helper tends to be more active than usual, attempting to clarify the situation, giving information or reassurance, and sometimes suggesting courses of action. In the midst of crises, most people are confused and uncertain of what to do. Often they need a caring helper who is not manipulative but who is willing to give support and direction until the people in crises are able to take over for themselves.

Table 7-1 Unhealthy and Healthy Ways to Meet a Crisis

Unhealthy Ways to Meet a Crisis	Healthy Ways to Meet a Crisis
1. Deny that a problem exists.	1. Face the fact that there is a problem.
2. Evade the problem by ignoring it, hiding it, or trying to escape it with alcohol or other drugs.	2. Attempt to understand the situation more fully.
3. Refuse to seek or accept help.	3. Open channels of communication with friends, relatives, pastors, or others who might be able to help.
4. Hide feelings of sorrow, anger, guilt, etc.	4. Face up to negative feelings of guilt, anxiety, or resentment, and consider actions and alternative ways of viewing the situation so that you can deal with these feelings.
5. Give no thought to practical ways by which the crisis might be handled.	5. Separate the changeable from the unchangeable in the situation, and accept that which cannot be changed.
6. Blame others for causing the crisis, and expect that somebody else is totally responsible for curing it.	6. Explore practical ways of coping with the problem, and take steps (however small) in handling the problem in a practical way.
7. Take on the role of a helpless victim who has been abused by others and who can do nothing except suffer.	7. Accept responsibility for coping with problems, even problems that seem to have arisen from situations beyond your control.
8. Turn away from friends or family.	8. Pray about the matter, honestly sharing your concerns with God. Remember that God is both aware of our crises and concerned about us.
9. Refuse to pray about the crisis.	
10. Convince yourself that a crisis is evidence of God's punishment or disfavor.	

There can be no standard formula or cookbook approach for helping a person in crisis, but some things can be done in almost every case.

Make contact
Christians believe that we can intervene from afar through prayer, and this must not be overlooked. But whenever possible we should also show personal concern by "being there," communicating compassion by our presence, warmth, and willingness to listen. The sooner we can be on the scene, the more likely we are to help. It helps, too, if you can maintain contact during the whole course of the crisis.

Reduce anxiety
This is not done by encouraging the helpee to think about something else. Sometimes we steer the conversation to other topics because we feel the need to reduce our own anxiety, but this doesn't do much to help people in crises. Often they want and need to talk about the situation, describe what happened, think back to happier times before the crisis, and feel free to express their emotions of sadness, grief, remorse, or anger.

At such times the helper can demonstrate calmness, concern, and acceptance. We can bring the comfort of the Scriptures and pray with helpees, making sure, however, that these are not gimmicks to keep them from talking about the hurt and expressing feelings.

If you don't know much about the situation, try to find out when the crisis started and what went on before it began. In doing this, you can sometimes spot the source of the trouble and begin to deal with it. If a person says, for example, that "everything was going great for me until I started college," we can assume that something in the college setting is causing the crisis symptoms.

Sometimes anxiety-reduction will involve bearing the brunt of the helpee's anger, helping him or her to see the problem more clearly, making positive comments about steps that have been taken to face the crisis, and helping the person in crisis to see that all is not hopeless. This, of course, can backfire if it is not done with sensitivity. Romans 8:28, for example, can be stated in a glib fashion so that the helpee feels angry, especially if he or she feels that the verse quoter has not taken the time to really understand the situation.

When several people are involved in a crisis, it helps if you can deal with the most anxious person first and send away the curious onlookers. Several years ago our family saw a little boy get hit by a car. As my wife, who is a nurse, applied first aid and talked calmly to the distressed mother, an older brother appeared on the scene. In an agitated manner, he yelled, "Mommy, is Jimmy going to die?" Immediately the whole scene got tense until my wife assured the older brother that Jimmy would probably be OK, and then suggested that the mother might want a coat or sweater over her shoulders as she rode in the ambulance. The older brother ran off to get the sweater, and the situation calmed down considerably.

Focus on the issues

In the midst of a crisis it is easy to see a mass of events, possibilities, and advice givers, all of which can be overwhelming. The helper can do several things at this point. First, help the person in crisis to explore the present situation by describing his or her feelings, thoughts, plans (if there are any), and efforts to solve the problem. This is a process of sorting out the problems one at a time, finding out what is threatening, and seeing what has been done or what might be done about the situation.

At some time there needs to be a narrowing down of what

the real problems are, an inventory of the person's resources (what money, ability, people, and opportunities are available), a listing of the different alternatives that the person might use, and an evaluation of each of these. If the helpee has not raised all of the alternatives, raise a few yourself. For each alternative, try to decide with the helpee what is feasible, what will really help with the problem, and what is easiest to accomplish.

Many years ago I visited a city where a number of homes had been damaged by a tornado. One house was completely destroyed except for a wall that was still standing. Across the wallpaper, in bold black letters, someone had written, "The Richardsons will build again!" Following the crisis their alternative had been decided!

Remember that people in crises are often very suggestible, so we must be careful not to push for our own solutions. The last thing a person in crisis needs is to experience failure. The fear of further failure immobilizes many people in times of crisis, so they need help and encouragement both in deciding what they should do and in making the decision to act.

In times of crisis, don't forget that your assistance may go beyond the crisis-victim whom you are trying to help. For example, you might be able to mobilize church or community aid. Massive prayer support not only can sustain a person through a crisis, but it can also be an encouraging demonstration that people really care. To this there might be added the more tangible help about which James writes: "Suppose a brother or sister is without clothes and daily food. If one of you says to him, 'Go, I wish you well; keep warm and well fed,' but does nothing about his physical needs, what good is it?" (James 2:15-16). Faith in Jesus Christ and commitment to him should show itself by the actions of caregiving Christians who help in tangible ways with money, supplies, babysitting, or other down-to-earth assistance.

Encourage action

Sometimes, with or without help, a person will decide on some course of action but will then be afraid to move ahead with the plan. Here is where a helper can encourage the helpee to acquire skills, if these are needed, and to take action. Be careful not to do things for the helpee all the time. When we face crises, it is easy for all of us to sit back and "let somebody else do it," and then to complain about the quality of service. People in crises need to be helped to help themselves. Each of these actions needs to be evaluated with the counselor's help, and if an earlier plan is unsuccessful, different or better alternatives need to be tried.

All of this assumes, of course, that the helper and helpee are the only ones involved in meeting the crisis situation. We should remember, however, that most crises begin with a series of environmental events or circumstances. Very often the most effective way to take action in a crisis is to change the environment. To help the helpee get another job, to mobilize the community to help rebuild a house or provide medical expenses, to counsel with relatives or friends who may have been causing much of the stress in the first place—these are all ways in which we can reduce the force of the crisis by making an intervention in the environment.

Help with acceptance

Often acceptance is a major step toward dealing with a serious problem. Sometimes a crisis will bring permanent change. The death of a loved one, the destruction of property, or the discovery of a terminal illness are examples of events that must be accepted. To do otherwise is to ignore reality, to deny the problem, and to delay the solution until later.

Acceptance, like healing, takes time. Often it involves a painful, conscious thinking about the situation, an expression of feelings, a readjustment of one's lifestyle, a building of new relationships, and a planning for the future. Acceptance may involve risks and potential failure. It is most successful when we are surrounded by sincere, patient, helpful friends, and when we know the Savior, who told us to come with our burdens and to cast them on him. Then we can experience the *peace* and *guidance* that give real *hope* and *stability* during times of crisis (Pss. 32:8; 55:22; Matt. 11:28-30). Remember that when a person casts his or her burden on the Lord, he may sustain us through other human beings—like the writer or readers of this book.

Jesus as a Crisis Counselor

In John 11 we see a familiar example of how Jesus helped people in a crisis that involved terminal illness, personal danger, and the loss of a loved one.

When Lazarus of Bethany became seriously ill, his sisters, Mary and Martha, sent a message to Jesus, but instead of hurrying to their need, he sat around for two days. Of course, Jesus knew what was going on in Bethany, and he even used the crisis to teach the disciples (vv. 4, 9-15) before they realized that the illness of Lazarus was terminal.

The disciples, in the meantime, were facing a crisis of their own. Not only was Jesus' life in danger but so were theirs because they were associated with a wanted man (vv. 8, 16). To appear in public was to risk violent death, but when Jesus told them that Lazarus was dead, they agreed to accompany the Lord to Bethany.

When they arrived, the scene was one of great sadness. Notice how Jesus handled the situation:

- He explained to the confused disciples what was happening (vv. 4, 14-15).
- He let Martha express her feelings and confusions (vv. 21-22).
- He reassured her in a calm manner and instilled hope (vv. 23, 25-26).
- He pointed her to the person of Christ (v. 25).
- He let Mary express her feelings, feelings that might have contained some anger (v. 32).
- He did not stop from grieving but, on the contrary, expressed his own sorrow (vv. 33-36).
- He calmly bore the hostility of many of the saddened mourners (v. 37), even though he was deeply moved by the whole situation (vv. 37-38).

Then Jesus took action—action that changed the sadness into joy, brought glory to God, and caused many people to believe in Christ (vv. 38-45). On this occasion Jesus did not send the observers away, as he had done at the raising of Jairus's daughter, but by calling Lazarus from the grave he demonstrated conclusively his victory over death, the greatest of all crises. A short time later, when he himself was executed, Jesus approached the Cross with calmness and then rose again. Little wonder the apostle Paul could affirm to the Corinthians that death had been swallowed up in victory and that believers had certainty of a life after death, a life with Christ himself (1 Cor. 15:51-58).

It is true that none of us can bring a dead person back to life as Jesus did, but it is also true that as crisis helpers we can employ each of the other techniques that Jesus used during this crisis in Bethany. Crises teach us to look more objectively at problems when they arise and to solve them more effi- ciently. This in turn contributes to our mental well-being and psychological stability. But crises also alert people to spiritual issues and teach us to lean more fully on the Christ who called Lazarus out of the grave. Everyone doesn't react this way, of course. Some get critical and angry with God, but others look back to crises as turning points in their spiritual journeys.

As we have seen, people in crises are often confused, suggestible, guilty, hopeless, and self-condemning. In situations like these, it would be easy for a helper to manipulate his or her helpee into making spiritual decisions that might be regretted, resented, or rejected at a later time.

Jesus did not resort to such tactics. When faced with the death of Lazarus and the danger to his own life, Jesus did not deny the spiritual implications of what was happening. He used the situation to teach spiritual truths, to show how to cope with crises, and to demonstrate the power of God in the lives of his children. Notice that in pointing to the spiritual he did not play on people's emotions, nor did he rob them of their freedom to doubt (John 11:16), to criticize (v. 37), to resist (vv. 46-53), or to turn to him and believe (v. 45).

God uses crises to bring people to himself. He uses crises to help Christians grow and to mature as disciples. Our task as people helpers is to be open to the leading of the Holy Spirit, trusting that he will show us when and how to bring spiritual issues into our crisis helping in a way that will draw the helpee closer to the Lord and ultimately bring glory to God.

CHAPTER EIGHT

Helping When People Are Desperate

WITHIN THE NEXT SIXTY SECONDS somebody in North America will attempt to take his or her life, and unless you are a speed reader, before you get to the end of this chapter at least one of these attempts will succeed. Chances are that the victim will be male, elderly, and depressed, although recent statistics show an alarming increase in suicide among teenagers and young adults. In the United States alone, an estimated two hundred thousand people attempt suicide every year. That's about twenty-three suicide attempts every hour. Every twenty minutes somebody succeeds. These suicides are very democratic. We see them in the rich and poor, the educated and uneducated, the young and old. And Christians attempt suicide along with unbelievers.

Consider John Baucom. His parents divorced and his father was murdered. Barely ten years old and distraught over the events in his family, the young man tried to take his own life. Writing many years later, after he had become a Christian psychologist, Dr. Baucom described what happened.

> I ran to my grandmother's kitchen and pulled out a large butcher knife. I wrapped my fingers around the handle, lifted the knife toward my chest, and began to stab myself. It seemed logical at the time. I would join my father and spend eternity with him. For some reason I felt no pain as the knife entered my side. A scream came from within me, although I didn't recognize my own voice. I recall my grandfather wrapping his strong arms around me. I began to sob almost convulsively as he held me to his chest. My body jerked as I slowly lost consciousness.
> Then I slept.
> I survived.
> The impact of that experience, however, lives with me. I'm certain it affects the way I relate to life today.[1]

The Nature of Suicide

Suicide is as old as recorded history. It is described in early Egyptian, Hebrew, and Roman writings, was discussed by the Greek philosophers, and has concerned writers and theologians throughout the whole Christian era. The Bible records seven suicides,[2] of which the death of Saul and the hanging of Judas Iscariot are probably the best known. Scripture never evaluates suicide, but the Bible clearly condemns murder, and to the extent that suicide could be considered self-murder, it is a sin against God. He created life through his Son (Heb. 1:1-3), he sustains life, and he—not we—has the sole right to end life.

For many people, however, there comes a time or times in life when crises are so bad and situations appear so hopeless that death seems to be the only way out. If you are involved in people helping, there is a good chance that someday you will be faced with a person threatening suicide. Your natural reaction may be to panic or to push the helpee off to someone else. Making a referral may be the best reaction in the long run, but sometimes this is not feasible, and occasionally it isn't even wise. Louis Dublin, who was a pioneer in suicide prevention, once remarked that the peer counselor probably is "the most important single discovery in the fifty-year history of suicide prevention. Little progress was made until he came into the picture."[3] Nonprofessional helpers have shown themselves to be very effective in helping people through the crises that lead to considerations of suicide. The nonprofessional, therefore, may be the most crucially important person in helping people who are contemplating self-destruction. For this reason, nonprofessional people helpers need all the knowledge they can get in spotting a potential suicide and deciding what to do about it.

When I was in the midst of writing this chapter, a man called a Chicago radio station and asked to speak to a disk jockey who was on the air. The caller was threatening to kill himself, so the radio announcer began asking questions to determine if the threats were real and if the man was serious. For three hours the DJ replaced his usual on-air commentary with music and talked to the man on the phone until help could arrive. At the end of this marathon session the radio personality reported that he felt exhausted and drained, but he had helped in a crisis situation when no professional helper was available. When he was asked later how he had known what to do, the disk jockey gave a simple answer.

"I know how it feels to seriously contemplate suicide," he said. "I was there once myself!"

For many years the police department in Los Angeles collected the suicide notes of people who had taken their own lives, but nobody paid much attention to these until two psychologists named Edwin Shneidman and Norman Farberow began to read and analyze them. Eventually this led to the establishment of the Los Angeles Suicide Prevention Center, where literally thousands of suicidal and potentially suicidal persons have been helped.

Based on the experiences of these and other counselors, we now know a great deal about suicide and suicide prevention.[4] Almost always, suicide is an attempt to find relief from intolerable psychological pain and a way to escape from a deep sense of hopelessness and helplessness. Suicide attempts often are cries for help—nonverbal ways of saying, "I'm under a lot of pressure and don't know what else to do." The helper's task is twofold: to judge how serious the person is about suicide and to take some kind of action based on this evaluation.

Evaluating Suicide Potential

Almost everyone who attempts suicide gives some clues of these intentions beforehand. Sometimes the clues are as clear as a person indicating that it might be good to "end it all" to escape a problem. More often, however, the clues are much more subtle and tend to be of five types: verbal (what the person says), behavioral (what the person does), descriptive (who the person is), situational (what has happened), and symptomatic (how the person is coping). In evaluating the potential for suicide, the helper must try to keep all of these in mind.

Verbal clues

These can be of two types. Sometimes the person comes right out and says that he or she is contemplating suicide. Such threats should be taken seriously. The old idea that "if he talks about it he won't do it" has no basis in fact.

The second type of verbal clue is more subtle. Statements

such as "I won't be at work next week" or "This is the last exam I'll ever study for" don't mention suicide, but they strongly hint that it is a possibility. Questions like "What could I do to help a friend who is thinking of killing herself?" might be a veiled clue to the questioner's own intentions.

Sometimes it is appropriate to ask a potential suicide victim if he or she has ever thought about specific methods. In general, if a person has thought about the time, place, and method, he or she is serious about these intentions, especially if the method is something like using a gun or jumping off a high balcony. These are almost always successful (assuming that the gun is loaded and the balcony high enough), unlike slashing one's wrists or taking a few extra aspirin tablets. If the person already owns a gun or has bought poison, the threat is even greater.

Behavioral clues

Sometimes people don't mention suicide, but their emotions and actions point in that direction. Consider, first, the emotions. Most people who consider suicide are depressed and feel that life is hopeless. Once they decide to kill themselves, however, they feel more relaxed. A decision has been made, some of the pressure has been lifted, and they show a sudden and noticeable change in mood. Often relatives are encouraged by this until the suicide attempt occurs.

Sometimes a person's actions reveal his or her intentions. Paying off old bills, updating insurance policies, giving away prized possessions like a stereo or golf clubs, and ceasing to communicate with a counselor are possible behavioral indications that the person is preparing to go away permanently.

Descriptive clues

These refer to who the person is, and, as such, they are clues that may or may not be helpful to the counselor. As we have seen, people of all ages and status commit suicide, but some are more prone to do so than others. In general, men commit suicide more often than women, although women make more attempts. Suicide is common in the elderly—some of whom have turned to controversial (and illegal) "doctor assisted suicide" in recent years. There also has been a dramatic rise in youthful suicides within the past decade or two. Among fifteen- to twenty-four-year-olds, for example, the rate of suicide has tripled since the mid-fifties and now ranks as the third most common cause of death for this age group (after accidents and homicide).[5]

To some extent the person's lifestyle is also important. Some people are chronic threateners. Like the little boy who cried wolf, they threaten often, although as they get older the likelihood of their carrying through increases. In general, however, threats from these people are not as serious as those that come from people who have had stable lives and marriages prior to the time of the suicide threat. These people can often be helped over a crisis, but at the time of their threat they are dead serious about suicide. They might just be dead if they are not watched carefully, taken seriously, and given help.

Situational clues

Before people start thinking about suicide there is usually some crisis or stress that they can't handle. Loss of a loved one, discovery of a malignancy or other serious illness (including AIDS), separation from children, loss of a job or status, divorce, despair over the inability to control drinking or sexual excesses, arrest, criminal involvement, destruction of property, loss of money—all of these can put a person under extreme stress. Even good things, like a promotion or graduation from college, are stressful to most people, although these rarely lead to suicide. Stress, therefore, must always be seen from the helpee's point of view, since he or she may view a situation much differently than we do. When the stress is intense, the likelihood of suicide is higher.

Symptomatic clues
The issue of how a person *copes* with stress is as important as the stress itself. Several symptoms indicate that a person is not coping very well. These indicators include depression and hopelessness, disorientation or confusion, a tendency to be complaining or dissatisfied, and sometimes a defiant attitude that says, in essence, "I may be down, but at least I'm in charge of ending my life when I please!" Alcoholics, drug addicts and other substance abusers, people who are termi-nally ill, and those who think they have a terminal illness may all be high suicide risks, especially if they feel overwhelmed by these conditions.

What about religion?
In the midst of all these depressing thoughts, it is refreshing to discover that among religious people, suicide is not as com-mon as it is among the nonreligious. Religious people even think less often about suicide, and when they are in the midst of stress, they are less inclined to attempt to end their lives.[6]

There may be several reasons for these conclusions. Along with families, the church often gives support in times of need or discouragement and enables us to solve or cope with prob-lems when they arise. In addition, most Christians believe in the sovereignty and power of God, and we know that he gives us a glimmer of hope even in the midst of difficult circumstances. Some Christians might also be dissuaded from suicide because they fear the displeasure of God if they take their own lives.

Even so, perhaps almost all readers of this book know of

Christians who have taken their own lives. When Christians show signs that they are thinking of suicide, we should take them seriously and be available to give help.

The Availability of Helpers

When a person is lonely, worried, and has no one to talk to, life is a lot more difficult, and suicide is much more likely, than if caring relatives and friends are nearby and willing to give help and support. But even when such friends are there, they can't help much if they have no indication that the person is thinking of suicide. Consider dentists, physicians, and lawyers, for example, all of whom have a higher-than-average rate of suicide even though they come into contact with people every day. Often these professionals lack other people to whom they can turn and honestly share struggles during times of stress.

In contrast, when there is someone to talk to, the likelihood of self-destruction is lowered considerably. Friends and relatives are the most obvious helpers, but as we have mentioned previously, there are others, including neighbors, coworkers, church members, pastors, teachers, family physicians, private counselors, or even barbers and hairdressers. These resource people can all help. So can the police dispatcher who answers an emergency call. So can the stranger who answers the phone at the suicide prevention center. So can you!

Table 8-1 is a summary of some of the more common suicide clues. It can be used as a checklist to determine how serious a person is about taking his or her own life. In general, the more check marks on your list, the greater the danger of suicide.

Preventing Suicide

For most of us, it can be scary to realize that at some time we might be talking with a person who is seriously

Table 8-1 Suicide Evaluation Checklist

Verbal
__ Open talk of suicide
__ Talk of not being present in the near future
__ Questions about suicide
__ No longer talking to a counselor

Behavioral
__ Severe depression (including apathy, insomnia)
__ Sudden improvement in mental attitude
__ Guilt, shame, embarrassment
__ Feelings of hostility, revenge
__ Tension and anxiety
__ Poor judgment
__ Knowledge of available methods
__ Clearly thought-out plans
__ Proposed method available (gun, drugs, etc.)
__ Giving away possessions
__ Buying or updating insurance
__ Paying long-standing bills
__ Putting personal affairs in order

Descriptive
__ One or more almost-successful past attempts
__ Sudden, first-time decision to kill self
__ History of instability or unstable family

Situational
__ Loss of loved person through death, divorce, separation
__ Loss of money, prestige, job (including retirement)
__ Serious illness, surgery, accident, loss of limb
__ Diagnosis of a terminal illness
__ Threat of criminal prosecution
__ Change(s) in life situation
__ Failure of counseling
__ Success, promotion, increased responsibilities

Symptomatic
__ Feelings of hopelessness
__ Dissatisfaction
__ Confused thinking
__ Tendency to complain
__ Defiant attitude
__ Drug or drinking problem
__ Inability to control impulses

Resources
__ No sources of support (friends, relatives, etc.)
__ Family, friends available but unwilling to help
__ Few or no religious beliefs
__ No church or community contact
__ Living alone

133

contemplating suicide. It is not unusual for a potential helper to conclude that he or she has not heard correctly, that the helpee is not serious, or that maybe the person will go someplace else with the problem. When a person communicates their intention before attempting suicide, some of the people who are best able to help instead respond with panic, fear, worry, and inactivity. By doing nothing they may hope to ignore the situation. But if the suicide takes place, these people, who perhaps could have helped but didn't, later feel guilt and self-condemnation.

The decision to commit suicide is an indication that someone is in a crisis. The crisis-intervention techniques discussed in chapter 7 can be useful in dealing with the suicidal helpee. Helpful, too, are your attempts to listen and respond with concern and honesty. Somebody has suggested that we also need "sharp eyes and ears, good intuition, a pinch of wisdom, an ability to act appropriately, and a deep resolve." This sounds simple, but it isn't specific enough to be of much use.

More helpful advice is given in a little pamphlet published by the Public Affairs Committee in New York. All the references are to men ("he" or "his"), but this applies to people of both sexes.

> *Do* take seriously every suicidal threat, comment, or act. Suicide is no joke. Don't be afraid to ask the person if he is really thinking about committing suicide. The mention won't plant the idea in his head. Rather, it will relieve him to know that he is being taken seriously, that he is better understood than he suspected.
>
> *Don't* dismiss a suicidal threat and underestimate its importance. Never say, "Oh, forget it. You won't kill yourself. You can't really mean it. You're not the type." That kind of remark may be a challenge to a suicidal person. Such a person needs

attention, not dismissal. Anyone desperate enough can be "the type."

Don't try to shock or challenge the person by saying, "Oh, go ahead and do it." Such an impatient remark may be hard to hold back if a person has been repeating his threats or has been bothersome to have around. But it is a careless invitation to suicide.

Don't try to analyze the person's behavior and confront him with interpretations of his actions and feelings during the moment of crisis. That should be done later by a professional.

Don't argue with the individual about whether he should live or die. That argument can't be won. The only possible position to take is that the person *must* live.

Don't assume that time heals all wounds and that everything will get better by itself. That can happen, but it can't be counted on.

Do be willing to listen. You may have heard the story before, but hear it again. Be genuinely interested, be strong, stable and firm. Promise the person that everything possible will be done to keep him alive, because that is what he needs most.[7]

Christian people helpers know that we are not alone in our helping activities. We have the Holy Spirit within who is a divine source of strength and wisdom, guiding us as we talk to troubled people. We need to be people helpers who pray for our helpees and for ourselves while we seek to be friends to those troubled persons who are trying to cope with crises. Often this friendship is the first step to witnessing, discipling, and showing the individual how he or she can have life in all its fullness (John 10:10) in spite of the present difficulties.

Making Referrals

Although peer counselors often are extremely helpful in preventing suicide and bringing people through crises, they will not be able to handle every problem that comes their way. No counselor can deal successfully with every problem; at times all of us will need to refer a helpee to some other person who is better able to deal with the problem. *One of the most significant ways we can help people is to refer them and sometimes take them to more competent sources of help.* To do this is not an admission of failure; it is a mature recognition that none of us can help everybody. Many people can get better assistance from someone with specialized training or expertise in an area where we lack competence. If we are really interested in helping people, we will not be resistant to the idea of making referrals.

Assume, for example, that we learn that a young man has taken an overdose of pills. Obviously we are not going to sit with him showing empathy and warmth. We need to get him to a hospital, contact his doctor if possible, and then try to get in touch with a relative. The immediate aim is to get medical attention as soon as possible. If we can't get to the person ourselves, we may have to call an ambulance, the police, or a local suicide prevention center and request their intervention.

This need to refer also occurs in less dramatic settings. Often our job is to provide short-term support and encouragement while we get the helpee to someone who can give better help. To do this, try to keep the answers to three basic questions in mind: When do I refer? Where do I refer? How do I refer?

When to refer
There was a time, several years ago, when professional counselors routinely suggested that all counseling problems should be referred. But when research began to show the effectiveness of peer counselors and the insufficient numbers of available professional helpers, many people began to conclude that referral might not always be best. Sometimes it is better

for the dedicated helper to stick with a helpee, perhaps with occasional advice from a more experienced professional or pastoral counselor.

Nevertheless, referral is necessary when the present helper lacks the time, stamina, emotional stability, or the skill and experience to continue the counseling. As a general rule, we should refer whenever we don't seem to be helping someone deal with a problem, when we are stuck and not sure what to do next, or when it is clear that our helpee is not changing and growing. More specifically, it is important to seek outside help for helpees who

- are in legal difficulties;
- have severe financial needs;
- require medical attention;
- are severely depressed or suicidal;
- appear to be losing control over behavior, thoughts, or emotions;
- require more time or emotional energy than we can give;
- want to shift to another counselor;
- show extremely aggressive behavior;
- make excessive use of alcohol or other drugs;
- have strong feelings of dislike, are sexually stimulated, or threaten the counselor;
- have a problem that appears to be getting worse in spite of your help;
- have problems that are beyond the helper's training or ability to help; and/or
- appear to be severely disturbed.

Sometimes it is easy to spot a severely disturbed person, but in other situations the disturbance is less obvious. One writer has given the following concise list of symptoms that may indicate the presence of a severe disturbance:

1. Persons believe (without any basis in reality) that others are attempting to harm them, assault them sexually, or influence them in strange ways.
2. They have delusions of grandeur about themselves.
3. They show abrupt changes in their typical patterns of behavior.
4. They hallucinate, hearing nonexistent sounds or voices, or seeing nonexistent persons or things.
5. They have rigid, bizarre ideas or fears that cannot be influenced by logic.
6. They engage in repetitious patterns of compulsive actions or obsessive thoughts.
7. They are disoriented (unaware of time, place, or personal identity).
8. They are depressed to the point of near-stupor or are strangely elated and/or aggressive.
9. They withdraw into their inner world, losing interest in normal activities.[8]

When symptoms such as these appear, referral would be a wise alternative.

Where to refer

Ministers and professional counselors often have a file of people and places to whom helpees can be referred. The peer helper usually lacks this information, but often we can get suggestions if we call an experienced local counselor. In remote geographical areas the range of choices may be limited, but in larger metropolitan centers the possibilities are almost endless.

Private practitioners, such as psychiatrists, psychologists, licensed professional counselors, and certified psychiatric social workers, often represent the first line of action. Do not limit your referrals to these professionals, however. Sometimes the helpee needs a good general practitioner, dentist, lawyer, or banker to help with a problem. And very often the needy person can get the greatest help from a pastor. Unlike most pastors, private practitioners often charge high fees, and this might have a bearing on where you refer. Remember, too, that professionals often unite together in clinics or groups that can provide diverse types of help.

Community agencies are another source of help. Some of these, such as mental health clinics, psychiatric hospitals, or outpatient psychiatric departments in a general hospital, deal primarily with personal problems. Marriage clinics, of course, deal with troubled marriages, and drug centers also have a specialized emphasis. Vocational guidance centers, employment agencies, legal aid societies, welfare agencies, and other social service agencies provide community help, often at minimal cost. Groups, such as the society for the blind or the local retarded children's society, should not be overlooked and neither should government agencies, such as the division of vocational rehabilitation or the department of welfare. The state welfare department often can provide guidance in finding referral sources within the government and without.

Lay organizations can also assist with referrals. Alcoholics Anonymous, for example, is often a good place to refer the problem drinker who wants help. Alcoholics Anonymous also has groups for the spouses and children of alcoholics. Within recent years a host of recovery groups have arisen to give support, guidance, and Twelve-Step programs of recovery for almost any problem that you will encounter. Diet programs seek to help people take off weight; groups such as Recovery, Inc. give support to former mental patients; and almost every city—at least in America—has a variety of self-help groups that are listed in the telephone book or known by church leaders. Within recent years many churches have given birth to support and recovery groups that have a clear Christian emphasis and that meet in private homes or in church buildings. This leads to an important question that faces Christian people helpers: How is religion viewed by the counselor or group to whom I make referrals?

We are making an unfair assumption if we conclude that all non-Christian counselors are opposed to religion and determined to undermine the faith of their helpees, but it is true that this sometimes does happen. It is also true that many Christian psychologists or other professionals may use a therapeutic approach that differs very little from the approach of non-Christian counselors. Since our desire is to see individuals become disciples and disciplers, it is difficult to see how progress can be made toward this goal if the counselor has purely secular goals, or if he or she has never heard about discipleship.

Let us not forget, however, that God is sovereign and powerful. He does not require people—including you and me—to have perfect theology before he uses us to touch lives. If we search the Scriptures, we find that God sometimes uses even nonbelievers to accomplish his divine purposes. A non-Christian counselor, such as a nonbelieving physician or lawyer, may at times use his or her professional skill to guide a helpee through a crisis or help restructure a personality, both of which get the person to a point of readiness to accept Christ and move toward becoming a disciple. Sometimes physical or psychological problems must be dealt with before we can come to the spiritual, and we have pointed out previously that all these aspects of the personality are important.

Nevertheless, to refer someone to a non-Christian or uncommitted counselor can be dangerous, and for this reason every attempt should be made to find someone who follows biblically based principles of therapy. To be realistic, we must recognize that such persons are rare and at times we will have to settle for a professional or support group that may not be Christian but that has a nonjudgmental attitude toward religion. God sometimes uses such people to bring about healing that ultimately allows the helpee to grow.

How to refer

Referral is not something that helpees always accept enthusiastically, especially if they specifically sought you to give them help and if a good relationship has developed. It is important, therefore, that the helpee not feel rejected or "passed off" to somebody else. To make the referral process as smooth as possible, several guidelines should be kept in mind.

First, involve the helpee in the decision to refer. Remember that the helper and helpee are coworkers, trying to solve problems together. You should decide jointly how the problems can be solved most effectively, and this may involve using another helper. If you are the first to bring up the referral idea, do so gently, giving the helpee plenty of time to respond.

Sometimes the helpee will be disappointed or angry with the idea of a referral. Often you can prevent this by suggesting to all of your helpees at the beginning that referrals sometimes are wisest. If you mention this early, long before a referral becomes necessary, then the idea is less disturbing or surprising when and if you raise it later.

Second, the helper can pave the way for referral by finding

out what community resources are available, what they cost, and whether or not they have a waiting list. It usually is better if the helpee makes his or her own appointment with the new counselor, although this is not a hard and fast rule.

Third, discuss the relationship that you will have following the referral. In professional circles, the former counselor usually takes a "hands off" attitude when the new counselor takes over. With pastoral or peer counseling, however, this isn't always necessary. There can still be contact, especially on a friendly, supportive or pastoral basis, though the new counselor or group usually will accept the major responsibility for helping.

Bible referrals

This whole idea of making referrals is as old as the Bible. Perhaps the most interesting example occurred when the children of Israel were camped at the foot of Mount Horeb in the middle of their wilderness travels (Exod. 18). Moses discovered that he was spending all of his time judging the people, hearing complaints, and settling disputes. Undoubtedly, this was mostly legal counseling, but perhaps some personal problems also were brought to Moses.

Jethro, Moses' father-in-law, was visiting at the time and watched all of this with increasing concern because Moses was apparently wearing himself out as a people helper (Exod. 18:18). Finally, Jethro intervened with some advice of his own. Choose some able, God-fearing helpers, Jethro suggested. Find people who are truthful, honest, available at all times, and willing to help with the counseling. When the problems get too difficult, these helpers will make referrals to a more experienced counselor (Exod. 18:26).

This is a good model for today. Skilled, Spirit-filled men and women of God have the privilege of helping each other.

But with this privilege goes the responsibility of referring difficult cases to others with greater expertise. To refer is sometimes the best way to help.

Notes

1. John Q. Baucom, *Fatal Choice: The Teenage Suicide Crisis* (Chicago: Moody, 1986), 2.
2. Abimelech (Judg. 9:53-54), Samson (Judg. 16:28-31), Saul (1 Sam. 31:1-6), Ahithophel (2 Sam. 17:23), Zimri (1 Kings 16:18), Saul's armor-bearer (1 Chron. 10:4-5), and Judas Iscariot (Matt. 27:3-5).
3. L. I. Dublin, "Suicide Prevention," in *On the Nature of Suicide,* ed. E. S. Shneidman (San Francisco: Jossey Bass, 1969).
4. For more detailed information about suicide, consult a good abnormal psychology book or technical publications such as the following: George E. Murphy, "Suicide and Attempted Suicide," sec. 71 in *Psychiatry,* ed. Robert Michels, et al. (Philadelphia: Lippincott, 1992); or Alec Roy, "Suicide," in *Comprehensive Textbook of Psychiatry,* fifth ed., eds. Harold I. Kaplan and Benjamin J. Sadock (Baltimore: Williams & Wilkins, 1989), 1414–27.
5. Robert C. Carson and James N. Butcher, *Abnormal Psychology and Modern Life,* ninth ed. (New York: HarperCollins, 1992), 412. For more information about youthful suicide, see Alan L. Berman and David A. Jobes, *Adolescent Suicide: Assessment and Intervention* (Washington, D.C.: American Psychological Association, 1991); or Anthony T. Mitchel, *Suicide: Knowing When Your Teen Is at Risk* (Ventura, Calif.: Regal Books, 1991).
6. Kenneth I. Pargament, Kenneth I. Maton, and Robert E. Hess, eds., *Religion and Prevention in Mental Health: Research, Vision and Action* (Binghamton, N.Y.: Haworth Press, 1992), 71–72.
7. C. J. Fredrick and L. Lague, *Dealing with the Crisis of Suicide.* Public Affairs Pamphlet 406A, New York, 1972.
8. Howard Clinebell, *Basic Types of Pastoral Care and Counseling,* rev. ed. (Nashville: Abingdon, 1984), 312–13.

CHAPTER NINE

Helping on the Telephone

I N THE MIDDLE of a high bridge in an eastern community, the local mental health center has mounted a telephone beneath a prominent sign that reads: "DESPERATE? Life *is* worth living! Pick up the HELPLINE. Available 24 hours a day."

I don't know if many despairing people have picked up that telephone and been dissuaded from leaping off the bridge. But we do know that "dial-for-help" helplines and other telephone counseling services have been in operation for many years since they were first introduced in England and Australia.

In 1958, when the Los Angeles Suicide Prevention Center was established, the founders turned to the telephone as an instrument through which people could be counseled. It has been estimated that there are now several hundred telephone counseling clinics in the United States alone. These include pastoral counseling, suicide prevention, poison control, teenage hotlines, drug information, pregnancy counseling, contact for the elderly, and a variety of other helpful services that the caller receives free via the telephone. In addition, literally thousands of radio call-in programs invite listeners to use the telephone to share their problems with professional counselors and other proclaimed experts who give advice over the air—between station breaks and interruptions for advertisements.[1]

Some professional counselors criticize this kind of caregiving and point out that there is no research to show that telephone therapy works.[2] But many people lack the courage or the funds to get counseling in person. It is easier and less threatening or embarrassing to talk by phone to a stranger. The caller is able to feel in control, it isn't always necessary to give one's name, and it is always possible to hang up. Often, callers will seek face-to-face counseling after they make the first step of talking to an anonymous telephone counselor. And for many people, especially the elderly and disabled who cannot get to a counselor's office, telephones are the only source of help.

The Uniqueness of Telephone Helping

Several years ago, during a lengthy visit to Switzerland, my family and I lived in a delightful chalet that did not have a telephone. This was a unique experience and one that was so relaxing that I tried—unsuccessfully—to talk my family into having our telephone removed when we got home. Some of the arguments I got in favor of keeping the telephone were most convincing: It is a means of keeping in touch with friends and relatives, it is almost indispensable in emergencies when one needs help in a hurry, and it is convenient for getting information or in making purchases. The worlds of business, education, and government would hardly survive without the telephone, and neither would most individuals—at least in developed countries like ours.

It is surprising, therefore, that telephone counseling is hardly ever mentioned in counseling books or journal articles, even though this may be one of the most common types of people helping. Telephone helping is convenient, especially in emergencies, and of great value to people whose lifestyles and problems hinder them from getting face-to-face counseling help. To be an effective people helper, the Christian should have some understanding of how telephone counseling works and should be aware of its limitations.

The Convenience of Telephone Helping

How many telephones are in your house? Probably you have more than one, and the chances are good that you even have more than one line and telephone number. We have come to realize that "help is as near as the phone," and for several reasons this makes telephone helping very convenient.

Telephone help is less threatening

When talking on the telephone, the helpee often feels less threatened because he or she is in control of the situation. It is the caller who dials the number in the first place, knowing that it is easy to hang up if he or she feels uncomfortable or doesn't like the helper's personality or questions. Often helpees feel more comfortable talking from the safety and security of their own homes rather than in some unfamiliar clinic office, church parsonage, or living room of a friend. For people who are afraid of being trapped by a counselor, a telephone is "the only way to go." It is a safe way to reach out for help.

Telephone help can be anonymous

The telephone also lets people remain anonymous. Some individuals are so threatened by face-to-face contact that they don't even want their names to be known. It is difficult to remain anonymous when you are talking to someone in person (although this sometimes happens on planes, when people pour out their troubles to a seatmate, secure in the knowledge that there probably will be no further contact after both passengers are swallowed up by the crowds and halls of the next air terminal). When you use the telephone, however, especially if you call a telephone clinic and talk to a stranger or if you call a radio talk show, you can talk about the intimate details of your life without risking rejection by someone who knows your identity. Even when friends are talking to one another, the telephone creates a safe distance. Back in my bachelor days I preferred to use the telephone whenever I asked a girl for a date because it was less embarrassing for me if I got turned down.

Telephone help is available

There are times when telephone counseling is the only available source of help. People who are sick and without transportation, or those who are many miles from a helper, can find that talking on the telephone is the most feasible way to get help. In the same way, the college girl who calls her mother to talk about problems may be using the best means at her disposal. People also use the phone when it would be inappropriate for a counselor to be present. A colleague of mine once received a call from a former student who had just been married. The couple was having some difficulties in sexual adjustment during the first night of their honeymoon, so they decided to call their old psychology professor, long-distance, at 2 A.M. (This really happened!). The professor gave them some encouragement and instruction in a situation in which telephone counseling, without doubt, was the best approach to take.

Telephone help saves time

So far we have mentioned the conveniences of telephones for the *helpee*, but this type of helping also has advantages for the *helper*, especially when the helper is a nonprofessional who is not concerned about things like fees or appointments. Telephone counseling can often save the helper the time and inconvenience of setting up an interview. He or she can use the telephone to "keep in touch" with helpees by giving them a frequent call to maintain contact and show interest. At times when the helper is unable to meet with a helpee personally, a brief telephone conversation may be all that is needed. This is especially true during periods of crisis when the helpee needs to know that someone cares, but when it is not practical to have daily interviews. The anonymous nature of telephone conversations can also be valuable in a different way:

> The telephone therapist . . . will be far more like the patient's ideal than the face-to-face therapist, since the patient is presented with only a part of the reality. On the telephone, we receive none of the visual clues about a person that we receive in face-to-face contact. We have no idea what the person we are talking with looks like, nor can we see facial expressions, and finally, we get none of the body language clues to his thoughts, feelings, and personality that we generally receive in a face-to-face contact. . . . The telephone contact, much more than the face-to-face interview, permits the patient to make of the therapist what he will . . . [and] what he *needs*.[3]

Emergencies and Telephone Helping

Telephone counseling is most helpful during *emergencies*. By using the telephone, a caller can get help fast, without going through all the rigmarole of setting up an appointment, traveling to a meeting place, or in the case of professional clinics, filling out forms and having one's name put on a waiting list.

A telephone call helps bypass these barriers. It can bring immediate help and put the caller in contact with someone who can instill hope and bring objectivity into a tense situation.

Many people have found that it is therapeutic to have someone whom they can call should the need arise. The teenager who knows that it is always possible to call the church leader or the basketball coach may never actually make the call, but he or she feels better because of the awareness that help is available should it ever be needed.

Whether or not they are facing an emergency, some people benefit from telephone counseling because their personalities won't let them get any other kind of help. People who live alone, for example, are sometimes unable to cope with intimate, face-to-face contacts with other people, but they may be able to talk on the telephone. Likewise, the person who is desperate often is confused and overwhelmed by circumstances, but a telephone contact may be a lifeline to getting help. Adolescents, for example, sometimes have difficulty admitting their vulnerability and need for help, but a telephone contact is less threatening and often directs them to the help they need.

Limitations of Telephone Helping

Counseling courses emphasize that the counselor should watch the helpee as well as listen to what he or she says. We can learn a lot about people by looking at how they are dressed, how they care for themselves physically, how they walk, or how they sit in the chair. Facial expressions, indications of tenseness, body movement, tears, or ways of breathing can all be important nonverbal clues that help us understand the helpee and build rapport more quickly. In addition, by observing gestures, head nods, and eye movements, the helpee can get a good indication of whether or not the helper is listening and trying to understand.

As soon as we start talking on the telephone, all of these visual clues are gone (at least until there is widespread use of "picture phones"), and this presents problems for everyone. Since he or she can't see the helper, the helpee doesn't know how the shared information is being received. As we have indicated, this is comforting to some helpees, especially if they are discussing embarrassing or sinful behavior. But it can also be comforting to know that the helper accepts you, is understanding, and is giving undivided attention to what is being said. The telephone caller doesn't see this, so the counselor must demonstrate his or her compassion and empathy verbally.

Like the caller, the telephone helper is also at a disadvantage. Cut off from nonverbal clues, he or she must listen very carefully not only to what is being said but also to such things as tone of voice, hesitations, changes in volume or speed or pitch, sighing, shakiness in the voice, or any other sounds that might reveal something about the helpee. If the caller is a stranger, it might be difficult to tell either the sex or age of the person, and of course, we have no clues about his or her grooming or nonverbal nervous mannerisms. Sometimes, therefore, we have to ask what we need to know—how old a person is, for example, or whether he or she is crying.

The helper's telephone manner also makes a difference. We need to use the "uh-huh" response occasionally to show that we are listening, and we need to project empathy, warmth, and genuineness through our words and tone of voice. A flat, disinterested monotone doesn't do much to show that we care. Once again, however, the value of "doing what comes naturally" must be emphasized. When helpers really care, their voices will convey this. If they couldn't care less, that will come through, too.

One other problem with telephone counseling is the tendency to engage in chatty conversation rather than in true helping. To some extent the difference between conversation and counseling isn't all that great. Chatting socially with a friend can often be therapeutic, especially for people who are lonely or in need of support, but counseling usually involves something more. There is a problem to be dealt with, and the helper must be objective and willing to confront, teach, or guide as necessary. This isn't always possible when a telephone call becomes no more than the social contact that we often associate with telephone conversations.

Practical Telephone Helping

An advertisement on a Philadelphia radio station urged people to call a telephone counseling service that promised to "cure severe shyness, panic attacks, and phobias of any kind" and to give help "with any other problem you might have." The advertisement aroused a storm of controversy among professional counselors who continue to challenge the idea that severe problems can be handled solely by telephone therapy.

Most people helpers would agree, however, that telephone helpers are able to communicate empathy and a willingness to understand the caller's problems. Often people need information, reassurance, hope in the midst of crises, guidance, and the realization that there is someone who cares. All of this is conveyed every day by people helpers who use the telephone.

Several years ago a published article gave some very down-to-earth guidelines for the person who counsels over the telephone. "You are limited only by your ingenuity," wrote the author. Within this limit you can do the following:

> You can listen. It may be a rare experience for the caller; he may learn something just from having the opportunity to talk

freely. . . . You can be yourself. People in a jam need other
people. You can mobilize resources, both in others and for
others. The caller often possesses the answer, or the where-
withal to create it, but cannot see it. You can help him find
his own answer, by helping focus the question to be
answered, for example. You can also mobilize resources for
him, in the sense of making referrals, making contacts with
other agencies, calling a friend or minister to the rescue, setting up an appointment in the morning, and so on.

You can learn your own limits and know when it is necessary to mobilize resources for yourself—when to yell for help.
Always err on the generous side in using your consultants. . . .
You can sympathize, question, clarify, suggest, inform, just
plain be there![4]

Despite its unique features there is much in telephone
counseling that is no different from any other kind of people
helping.

Be alert to the helpee's problems
This involves asking yourself, Why is he or she on the phone?
What kind of help is needed? What can I do? Very often, of
course, we don't know what the real problem is, so we guess
and then try to get facts that will prove or disprove our
hypothesis. In time a clearer picture of the problem will
emerge.

Be sensitive to the helpee's feelings
How is he or she responding emotionally? Is the caller
depressed, anxious, embarrassed, defensive, angry, suspicious,
or expressing hope? Does he or she seem unusually placid
or emotionless? What about the intensity or appropriateness
of feelings? In all of this, the helper keeps pondering what
these feelings might mean or what they might tell about
the helpee.

Be aware of the helpee's thinking

What is the caller's problem? Does he or she have any ideas about what might be causing the problem or how it can be dealt with? What has been tried in the past? As the helpee talks, be alert to such signs of tension as rambling speech, lack of clarity, inability to concentrate, or a tendency to jump to faulty conclusions. Remember that God made us rational creatures but that we often don't think very rationally, especially when we are under stress. *What* a person thinks and *how* one thinks can both be clues to the nature of a problem.

Be sensitive to the helpee's actions

Sometimes problems come because of the words, actions, or sinful behavior of other people, but at times a problem is one's own fault. We may take a "poor little me; no one cares" attitude and complain that we are victims of fate or of other people's insensitivity, whereas it may be that our own attitudes and actions are driving people away and making us miserable. Not all problems are our own fault, but many are. Sin can get us into trouble and so can inconsistent behavior and actions that are self-defeating. A lady who feared that she was losing her married daughter attempted to prevent this by reaching out in a smothering and demanding way. Naturally, the daughter resisted this and drew back. The mother, in turn, became more demanding of love and attention, so much so that she eventually drove her daughter away. By her own actions the mother brought about the result that she feared most.

Be alert to common counselor errors

Helping on the telephone has several traps that we should try to avoid. Many of these are encountered as well in face-to-face counseling. Consider, for example, the tendency to over-emphasize questions. Perhaps this is the easiest trap to get into. Almost from the beginning you can get into a question-answer routine that leaves you desperately trying to think of new questions to ask so you can keep the interview moving. The helpee, in turn, begins to assume that you will come up with a concise diagnosis of the problem and with answers to his or her questions once you get all of this information. As we have seen, it is better to ask open-ended questions—the kind that cannot be answered in a word or two. "What's been happening lately?" or "What kinds of feelings have you been having?" are better than asking, "Are you depressed?" Keep the language simple, and don't be afraid to use prodding comments, such as "Tell me more," "What happened then?" or "That must have aroused some feelings in you."

Another common error is an overeagerness to find quick solutions. The helpee may have been struggling with his or her problem for a long time, so why should you think it is possible to solve everything in ten or fifteen minutes? It is better to take your time and to put most of the initial emphasis in listening.

It helps, too, if the counselor avoids clichés. Normally these are used in good faith, but they can be very annoying. "I know just how you feel," "Don't worry about it," "You'll get over it," "Remember that all things work together for good," "Just pray about it" are all statements that are not very helpful to people under tension. Sometimes these clichés are accompanied by a little sermon or capsule of advice. Invariably these are well meant, but they are seldom heeded, and more often than not they reflect insecurity on the part of a helper who doesn't know what else to do or say.

Surprising as it may seem, helpers and helpees sometimes make the error of avoiding a problem altogether. It hurts to talk about the helpee's marriage breakup, job failure, or rebellious kids, so we sometimes talk about the weather, sports, or politics instead. Several years ago somebody gave me a delightful little metal figurine of a counselor sitting in a chair with a helpee on the couch. I put this on my desk but soon discovered that it was more than a conversation piece. It was a good topic for discussion that didn't build rapport (as I had hoped) as much as it became a distraction from the more painful but necessary discussions of the helpee's problems.

Games People Helpers Play

Many years ago a psychiatrist named Eric Berne wrote a popular book that he entitled *Games People Play*. Borrowing from Berne, we might list some games that people helpers play—whether or not they are talking on the telephone.[5]

Game 1. "I've got to say something." This attitude says we have to come up with a quick answer, even though such answers are often superficial and unrealistic. It is better to listen longer.

Game 2. "I better not say what I'm thinking, or it might happen." This borders on superstition. It is the idea that we shouldn't raise issues of suicide, possible failure, death, or the possibility of the helpee's being sued for divorce, lest this shake the helpee and/or cause the feared event to happen. Helpees are rarely that sensitive. If a helper thinks of some pending crisis, the helpee probably has thought of it, too, and might appreciate the chance to discuss the issue openly.

Game 3. "If only I knew more, I could help." This may hide a fear of failure in the helper who, in turn, searches for more information, or perhaps a biblical proof-text that will be a key to unlocking the problem and bringing instant mental health. People helping is hard work. Together the helper and helpee must look for answers, but it is rare to find a nugget of insight so golden that it solves the problem quickly and efficiently.

Game 4. "There must be an answer if only I can think of it." There can be great frustration if we try to come up with a directive, authoritarian solution to every problem. Our job is to be the Holy Spirit's instrument in helping troubled people. Often he will lead us to a passage of Scripture or to a biblical principle that speaks directly to the problem, but this does not always happen. There are no pat answers to many of the issues that we encounter as people helpers, so our goal is to be available so that the Holy Spirit works through us to bring change and healing that is in accordance with the teachings of Scripture.

Game 5. "There must be somebody who can help." Probably this is true, and for that reason referral is often wise. Remember, however, that in many situations lay counselors can be effective; the helpful "somebody" might be you.

Game 6. "I am an empathetic, warm, understanding, and consistently competent counselor." This is what all of us want to be, but in reality we are fallible human beings who sometimes make mistakes, including serious counseling errors. When this happens, we ask the Lord to forgive us, often ask our helpees to do the same, and go on determined not to make the same mistake again.

Handling Problem Callers

Telephones are available twenty-four hours a day, and this can create havoc if you answer the phone whenever it rings. Answering machines can help you screen calls, but even then it is difficult to handle what might be labeled the subtle, chronic, silent, or obscene callers.

The subtle caller
This person really wants help but lacks the courage or willingness to come right out and admit a problem. Sometimes,

for example, these people say they are calling to talk about the problem of a friend. It is best to accept this at face value, especially at first, but often the "friend" is really the person who is making the call. At other times, you might get a call for information about suicide, pregnancy, AIDS, depression, or some other topic. Once again you can assume that these are legitimate requests for information, but it may be the caller who has the problem. On occasion a caller may hang up when you answer, perhaps because he or she loses courage or wants to check out your tone of voice before speaking. Often these people call back later.

At times callers are hostile or inclined to joke about people, like themselves, who call for help. This may be a defense that reflects their discomfort. By reacting in a gracious or serious manner, the counselor can get to the problem more quickly.

Taken together, subtle callers are those who speak on one level but who really hope to get help, sympathy, and understanding for problems that they have not been able to bring up. These subtle approaches are not limited to telephone counseling. They often occur in face-to-face people helping as well.

The chronic caller

The chronic caller is the person, often lonely or depressed, who calls several times every day. This, of course, can be draining on the helper and difficult to handle. We could tell such people not to call at all, or alternatively, we could give them only partial attention as they talk on for as long as they want every time they call. In both cases we are not likely to help, and such responses can lead to guilt or frustration in ourselves. It is better to set limits, perhaps by stating that calls must be limited to ten minutes and then sticking to this rule. Sometimes chronic callers can be put in touch with each other or with peer helpers in the church who have more time to listen.

At times you might also suggest "writing therapy" in which the caller writes about the problems and mails in these letters instead of talking. This is worth a try, although people who like to talk incessantly often want the human contact that letter writing does not give. If you reduce contact with a caller like this, you might want to call periodically to give the reassurance that you care. Try not to feel guilty about setting some limits on the time or number of calls. This helps the caller face reality and contributes to the greater well-being of counselors and the family members with whom they live.

The silent caller
The silent caller presents a different kind of problem. This person is motivated enough to call but refuses to say much once you are on the phone. As a result, you are cut off from both visual and auditory clues. In times like this you could read your mail or skim a magazine—since the caller can't see you—but it is better to give encouragement. Possible prompts include comments such as "Sometimes it's difficult to talk, isn't it?" "Is there something I can do to help?" or "It's hard to know what's happening when you don't talk." When all else fails, you might try a response such as "I'd like to talk with you, but I'll have to hang up in a minute or two if you can't talk." If there is still silence, you might assure the caller of your interest and God's concern, encourage him or her to call again at some other time when it might be easier to talk, then say good-bye before hanging up.

The obscene caller
The obscene caller especially enjoys calling church leaders because he (usually these callers are men) likes to shock such people and see if he can get them angry. If he can get a

preacher mad, it proves to him that religious people aren't so good and that probably they are as bad as the media often suggest. In a strange way this contributes to the caller's self-esteem, as does the feeling that swearing is a way to assert masculinity or one's power over other people. Getting mad at such callers is not the way to handle this situation, but neither is it appropriate to listen with "unconditional positive regard." Firmness, mixed with kindness and compassion, is the best approach. "I'm glad to talk with you," we might say, "but I'll have to ask you not to use that kind of language." If the caller persists, threaten to hang up, then do so. If the calls continue, the local police or telephone company should be contacted. Remember that such callers have problems, and their calls may be a hidden cry for help and understanding.

Discipleship and the Telephone

For obvious reasons, Jesus never used the telephone in his ministry, but for us, the telephone, like radio and television, is an instrument that gives a greater opportunity to intervene in the lives of others. Like face-to-face helping, telephone helping has the same discipling goals. It is unlikely that few, if any, people will be discipled completely over the phone, but technically this is possible. The telephone can be used to give encouragement, support, advice, guidance, and confrontation. The gospel can be presented over the phone, we can pray with people over the phone, and we can encourage them in their personal and spiritual growth. Shut-ins or disabled helpers can have a special telephone ministry, using the phone to go where they cannot go in person.

Telephone helping must not be overlooked by those whose ultimate goal in life is to fulfill the Great Commission by going into all the world to make disciples. Part of our going can well be through the telephone.

Notes

1. There is no debate about the popularity of these call-in programs, but there is disagreement about whether counseling by telephone plus radio really works to bring change. See Berkeley Rice, "Call-in Therapy: Reach Out and Shrink Someone," *Psychology Today* (December 1981): 39, 41, 44, 87–91; and Amiram Raviv, Alona Raviv, and Ronith Yunovitz, "Radio Psychology and Psychotherapy: Comparison of Client Attitudes and Expectations," *Professional Psychology: Research and Practice* 20 (April 1989): 67–72.

2. James Buie, "Therapy by Telephone: Does It Help or Hurt?" *APA Monitor* (1989): 14–15.

3. T. Williams and J. Douds, "The Unique Contribution of Telephone Therapy," in *Crisis Counseling and Counseling by Telephone*, by D. Lester and G. W. Brockopp (Springfield, Ill.: Charles C. Thomas, 1973), 85.

4. C. W. Lamb, "Telephone Therapy: Some Common Errors and Fallacies," *Voices* 5 (1969–70): 45–46.

5. Adapted from Lester and Brockopp, Part III. Eric Berne, *Games People Play* (New York: Grove Press, 1964).

CHAPTER TEN

Helping in the Church

URING HIS MINISTRY on earth, Jesus was
very much concerned about healing. In talking to some critics
he made the oft-quoted comment that he had come not to
minister to people who were well. He had come for those who
needed to be healed (Mark 2:17). In the Gospels more attention is given to the healing ministry of Jesus than to any other
subject except the events surrounding the Crucifixion and
Resurrection. In the first five books of the New Testament,
one fifth of all the verses deal with healing.[1]

These biblical healings almost always took place in the
presence of other people and often at the request of others.
Sometimes concerned friends or relatives brought the sick
person to Jesus, but at other times they requested healing
when the person in need was not even present.

In the preceding pages we have talked about psychological-
spiritual healing and about helping as an interaction between
two people—the helper and the person being helped. We

know, of course, that counselors sometimes work in pairs and that people are often helped in small group settings. But even when several people are involved, the helping usually comes from within the small group. Outsiders rarely participate in the healing process. Is it possible, however, that helping can be more effective when it takes place within the setting of a larger community of concerned people?

Helping in Groups

Psychologists discovered the effectiveness of group helping many years ago. Mental patients who had been chained in unsanitary asylums were found to improve dramatically when they were treated with compassion and kindness. As part of something called "moral treatment," the hospital administrators and staff lived with the patients, ate with them, and showed that the hospital could be a therapeutic community instead of a prisonlike dungeon.[2] This idea was extended further after World War II, when a British psychiatrist named Maxwell Jones proposed a therapeutic community in which all of the patient's daily activities were directed toward his or her recovery. *Milieu therapy* was a term that applied to this kind of treatment. Oneto-one counseling was part of the treatment, but equally important was the daily support, help, and encouragement given by the staff and the patients to each other.

Milieu therapy made a number of interesting assumptions about the helping relationship. First, it assumed that there was therapeutic value in activities such as living in a community, working, participating in recreational activities, and being part of support-giving encouragement groups. Second, milieu therapy built on the assumption that patients got better faster when the ward had an atmosphere of openness, honesty, warmth, acceptance, and interpersonal caring. All patients and staff were expected to treat one another with courtesy and consideration. Third, milieu therapy encouraged a "do-it-yourself" attitude. There was little emphasis on the idea that we are helpless victims of our pasts but a lot of focus on taking responsibility—for making decisions, keeping the hospital clean, planning ward activities, dealing with one's own problems, and even evaluating one another's progress. A fourth assumption was that all the staff were of value and equal importance. Ward aides and psychiatrists were both respected and listened to. There was to be open communication between the people on the ward. Disagreements were neither hidden nor squelched but were dealt with in a straightforward way.

All of this may sound idealistic, but research has demonstrated that milieu therapy leads to a greater overall improvement than other more traditional forms of treatment. And when the patients leave the hospital following milieu therapy, they are less likely to return—especially if they have been taught social skills and stress management as a part of their treatment.[3]

Therapeutic groups and communities

The value of a therapeutic or healing community to back up and sometimes replace individual counseling has become widely accepted since Jones first wrote about milieu therapy. Group counseling is now used by many counselors, in part because it is less expensive for the group participants. More often, however, groups are used because there is proven therapeutic value for people who come together to encourage and help one another. This helps to account for the explosion of interest in self-help and recovery groups.

Many psychological writers and small-group leaders fail to realize that Jesus and the New Testament writers gave a model of the ideal healing community many centuries ago. The assumptions of moral and milieu therapy were first stated in the Bible, but for some reason Christians have failed to follow the scriptural model. As a result, many churches have neglected their roles as therapeutic or helping communities. Instead, some local churches have become listless organizations where counseling is left to the pastor or a few laymen and where people in need of help are often ignored or rejected, especially if they are not active church members or do not show socially acceptable mannerisms, dress, behavior, or religious language.

The Nature of the Body of Christ

When Jesus was on earth, he ministered through his own physical body. Wherever he went, he touched, healed, counseled, showed compassion, taught, and lived a life that was a model for others to follow. When he went back to heaven following the Resurrection, his physical body disappeared from Earth, but Jesus left another body to carry on his work. This new body of Christ, which still exists today, is the church.

A faulty view of the church

Modern men and women have developed faulty views of the church. Many see it as an irrelevant organization of pious or hypocritical people who believe in God but who mainly are concerned about adding members, developing programs, politicking in the society, and erecting bigger and bigger buildings that stand vacant for most of the week.

Several insightful books, some written by psychologists and sociologists, have shown the weaknesses and insensitivities of many churches. We have learned, for example, that churches can abuse, can perpetuate myths, and can inject members with toxic faith.[4] One of my most respected friends, a theologian whose adult life has been dedicated to building healthy churches, once wrote about his own frustrating experiences of attending church as a young man and returning home livid with anger.

> It seemed that almost everything that took place in most churches was devised to kill the spirit of believers and to deaden vital Christians. As for unbelievers, it seemed that every aspect of church life had been calculated so that, if perchance an outsider had wandered in, he or she would be discouraged from ever setting foot in the place again. It was as if the *ideals* that were assiduously pursued were *tedium, inertia, mediocrity, rigidity,* and *close-mindedness*—and all in the name of Christ who had actually established the church in the world to turn it upside down!
>
> It occurred to me that the church had unthinkingly become captive to irrelevant traditions and to worldly values that stifled the energies, the gifts, and the dreams generated by the Spirit. Where the gospel teaches that everyone matters to God and that Christ died for all, many churches claim that Christ died only for them, and the rest of the world be damned. Where the gospel proclaims God's forgiveness and acceptance, many preach condemnation and rejection. Where the gospel brings a message of hope, they preach a message of doom. Where the gospel grants freedom in Christ, they impose man-made rules and regulations. Where the gospel requires every believer to do ministry, they watch their minister do everything. Where the gospel is a force, they make it a farce.[5]

A biblical view of the church

Clearly this is far from the model of the church described in the Bible. The church is supposed to be a body of believers who have committed their lives to Jesus Christ and have been equipped with spiritual gifts that each person discovers and develops (Eph. 4; 1 Peter 4:10). These gifts, listed in Romans 12, 1 Corinthians 12, and Ephesians 4, include such things as teaching, evangelizing, helping, exhorting (which, as we have seen, is very similar to counseling), healing, showing mercy, giving, and others. Spiritual gifts come directly from the Holy Spirit, who gives according to his will (1 Cor. 12:11).

Ephesians 4:12-13 states that the gifts of the Spirit have two purposes. First they are to prepare individual believers for service as a part of the body of Christ. Jesus came to evangelize, to enlighten, to release those who were in bondage, and to proclaim the truth (Luke 4:18). The modern body of Christ has a similar function. Just as the Holy Spirit empowered Jesus (Luke 4:18), so the Spirit also empowers us and gives gifts that enable us to minister to one another.

The second purpose of spiritual gifts is to build up the body of Christ so we can be unified, knowledgeable, and mature men and women. Such people are not tossed about by the most recent fad, psychological therapy, or philosophy of life. They are knowledgeable, stable, loving people whose lives are centered in Christ (Eph. 4:12-16).

The authentic people helper

What does all of this have to do with being an authentic people helper? The answer is this: One of the major purposes of the body of Christ, the church, is to help people. "God has combined the members of the body . . . so that there should be no division in the body, but that its parts should have equal concern for each other. If one part suffers, every part suffers with it; if one part is honored, every part rejoices with it. Now you [that is, believers] are the body of Christ, and each one of you is a part of it" (1 Cor. 12:24-27). According to God's plan, the church is to be a united body of believers who are given power by the Holy Spirit, are growing to maturity, and are ministering to (i.e., helping) people both inside and outside of the body.

People Helping and the Body of Christ

The body of Christ exists for a number of purposes, all of which are very beneficial to individuals, including our helpees. When it is functioning as it should, the body praises God through worship, builds people through the fellowship that it provides, and reaches out through service, including evangelism.[6]

Helping through worship

Most of us have experienced worship services that are boring, poorly planned, predictable, uninspiring, and focused more on the worship leader than on God. But worship can be a coming together of believers who are united in acknowledging and celebrating the nature of God and his centrality in all of life.[7] By meeting with others to sing, pray, receive instruction, read Scripture, give, and meditate together, we let our minds dwell on God, thank him for his attributes and his actions, and acknowledge that we are part of the family of God.

Most of the problems that people helpers encounter are problems faced by individuals. Individuals struggle with anxiety, loneliness, low self-esteem, failure, stress, and disappointment. Even marital problems and other interpersonal struggles most often involve only two or three people. When we come to worship, however, we are surrounded with other believers, many of whom are fellow strugglers. Together we acknowledge that God is still powerful and ultimately in control, and we find strength and comfort as the Holy Spirit brings comfort and reassurance in the midst of other believers.

I have a friend who works as a counselor in a large downtown church. During the course of the week he sees a lot of hurting people whom he counsels one by one. But he only sees people who agree to supplement the counseling by joining a small group and by attending worship services regularly. My friend has learned that people who worship together often find strength, support, and healing as they turn their attention to God in the presence of other Christians.

Helping through fellowship

Many people in need of help are lonely and longing for some kind of in-depth fellowship with another human being. This kind of fellowship is exactly what the body of Christ provides. Believers have fellowship with the God of the universe (according to the Bible, this automatically leads to joy) and with one another (1 John 1:3-4, 7). This kind of fellowship, which characterized the early church, arose because people had a common commitment to Christ (1 Cor. 1:9). Such a commitment and closeness ought to exist today. In many churches it does.

The body of Christ has tremendous potential for providing the kind of fellowship, acceptance, feeling of belonging, and security that brings great therapeutic value, both to believers and to other needy people who come into contact with believers. The New Testament uses the Greek word *koinonia* to describe this kind of fellowship. It involves Christians sharing together, bearing one another's burdens, confessing faults to each other, mutually submitting, encouraging one another, and building each other up as we walk with the Lord. In one word, Christian fellowship is the continual expression of *love.*

Several years ago Harvard psychologist Gordon Allport called love "incomparably the greatest psychotherapeutic agent." He suggested that the church knows more about this than any secular counselor, but he decried the "age-long failure of religion to turn doctrine into practice." [8]

The body of Christ should be characterized by love—love for ourselves, our neighbors, our families, and even our enemies. Jesus loved us and died for us even while we were still sinners (Rom. 5:8). If this divine love were to flow through Christians and reach out to others, like it should, the results would be incredibly therapeutic.

But to love like this is difficult and risky. It takes time and effort, and we might be inconvenienced. Too often, therefore, we talk about love but do very little about it.

But love is the basic mark of a Christian (John 13:35), and we are instructed repeatedly to be loving people (e.g., Matt. 22:39; 1 Thess. 4:9-10). The biblical description of love as recorded in 1 Corinthians 13 presents a high standard. "Love," we read, is "very patient and kind, never jealous or envious, never boastful or proud, never haughty or selfish or rude. Love does not demand its own way. It is not irritable or touchy. It does not hold grudges and will hardly even notice when others do it wrong. It is never glad about injustice, but rejoices whenever truth wins out. If you love someone, you will be loyal to him no matter what the cost. You will always believe in him, always expect the best of him, and always stand your ground in defending him" (1 Cor. 13:4-7, TLB).

When we and our helpees are members of communities where that kind of love is experienced and given, people helping is much more effective. In contrast, genuine and long-lasting people helping is far less possible, and perhaps even impossible, when we seek to give our assistance apart from the fellowship that is found in the body of Christ.

Helping through service

When Jesus was asked how a person could be great, his reply was somewhat surprising. The way to be great, he said, is to become a servant (Matt. 20:26; Mark 9:35). This idea comes up repeatedly in the New Testament. Christians are to be submissive to one another and to serve one another.

This is an *other-centered* rather than a *self-centered* way of living. It is a lifestyle that, if practiced consistently, would lead to a series of mutual helping relationships. It would cause all Christians to be concerned about bearing one another's burdens (Gal. 6:2), weeping and rejoicing together (Rom. 12:15), confessing sins to each other, and praying for one another (James 5:16).

"At no time does the church resemble more the Savior than when it emulates him in self-giving servanthood in response to situations of human need," writes Gilbert Bilezikian in *Christianity 101.*

> During his ministry, Jesus viewed himself as fulfilling a servant role among God's needy creatures, and he commissioned the disciples to do likewise. He was overwhelmed with compassion whenever he came across the sick and the blind (Matt. 4:24; 20:34), the oppressed, the helpless (9:36), and the hungry and the bereaved (15:32; Luke 7:13). He entered into their pain and, as a result, he was moved to action, dispensing relief, comfort, and healing. (p. 217)

Needy people often lack the energy and emotional stamina to be giving this kind of service to others, and every counselor knows that some people give out of self-centered motives. But when people, including needy people, are willing and able to give as a genuine expression of caring, the greatest benefits often come to the givers. Jesus said that it is more blessed to give than to receive (Acts 20:35). Sometimes the giver receives blessing in the form of greater feelings of stability and well-being.

The body of Christ is to be a growing, maturing group of people. They are not to be like children, but instead they are to grow together as a working unit, becoming more and more like Christ, who is head of the body (Eph. 4:13-16). Consider what this kind of community could do for the person who needs help. It could

- provide a sense of belonging or fellowship;
- show an interest in and prayerful concern for the helpee, his or her helper, and their relationship;
- provide practical and tangible help for people in need;
- give opportunity for the person in need to serve others (this is good therapy);
- show a biblical love to people who don't feel loved but need it;
- provide a meaningful philosophy of life;
- support and guide individuals and families in times of crises;
- provide accountability;
- encourage confession of sin and commitment to the sovereign Christ;
- give advice and encouragement to the helper when he or she faces difficult counseling situations;
- guide individuals toward maturity in their relationships with Christ;
- encourage the helpee as he or she develops new behavior;
- provide a variety of models of maturity and psychological-spiritual stability; and
- accept sufferers, including former alcoholics,

prisoners, mental patients, and others who feel unwelcome in the community as a whole.

The Helping Body

From the time it began, the body of Christ, the church, has been a helping community. There has been isolation, insincerity, inactivity, backbiting, noncooperation, dishonesty, rigidity, and a host of other pagan practices in the church, but there has also been a small "company of the committed" who have built their local churches on New Testament principles. These are the congregations that most likely have demonstrated the four helping actions of the church: healing, sustaining, guiding, and mending broken interpersonal relationships.

To be a true helping community that it was meant to be, the church first must return to the biblical pattern of *every* member committing his or her life to Christ, developing individual spiritual gifts, and actively using these (including the gift of *helping)*) to minister to others as we move toward Christian maturity. Individuals who work at this on their own can and often do help people. But the body working as a unit is much more desirable and effective in really helping others.

Second, we must remember that the body as a whole can take specific actions to meet human needs. The church can *encourage and pray* for helpers and helpees, can *give tangible help* to those in need (even to those with so-called taboo problems), can *provide a stable and accepting community* for members and visitors, and can *support* the repentant or cured individual who is making his or her way back into society. By doing this the body of Christ performs both therapeutic and preventive helping. This is an effective kind of help because it is peer helping, it is mutual helping, and it is helping centered around Jesus Christ, the head of the body.

Notes

1. Morton T. Kelsey, *Healing and Christianity* (New York: Harper & Row, 1973), 14.
2. J. S. Beckeven, *Moral Treatment in American Psychiatry* (New York: Springer, 1963).
3. Some of the research is summarized briefly by Robert C. Carson and James N. Butcher in *Abnormal Psychology and Modern Life,* ninth ed. (New York, HarperCollins, 1992), 683–84.
4. For example, see Stephen Arterburn and Jack Felton, *Toxic Faith: Understanding and Overcoming Religious Addiction* (Nashville: Oliver-Nelson, 1991); Ronald M. Enroth, *Churches That Abuse* (Grand Rapids: Zondervan, 1992); or Andrew Greeley, *The Catholic Myth: The Behavior and Beliefs of American Catholics* (New York: Scribner's, 1990).
5. Gilbert Bilezikian, *Christianity 101: Your Guide to Eight Basic Christian Beliefs* (Grand Rapids: Zondervan, 1993), 176.
6. I have discussed the following material in more depth in my book, *The Biblical Basis of Christian Counseling for People Helpers* (Colorado Springs, Colo.: NavPress, 1993), 195–211. Also see chapter 7 of Bilezikian's book, or John F. MacArthur, Jr., *The Master's Plan for the Church* (Chicago: Moody, 1991).
7. Adapted from Bilezikian, *Christianity 101,* 203.
8. Gordon W. Allport, *The Individual and His Religion* (New York: Macmillan, 1950), 90, 93.

CHAPTER ELEVEN

Helping by Prevention

THE PREVIOUS PAGES have reminded us that sensitive, willing helpers can greatly assist others as they cope with problems, deal with crises, and learn how to get along better. But sometimes people helping has nothing to do with crises or emotional problems. Helping a friend move, watching the neighbor's kids for an afternoon, or assisting a fellow student with a term paper are all helpful acts that make life a little easier for someone else.

Another type of helping is discussed in this chapter. Often overlooked by counseling books, it is every bit as important as the more traditional forms of people helping. Professional counselors give it names like *preventive psychiatry* or *community psychology*, but it has a clear purpose: to prevent the problems and crises that people often bring to counselors.

The prevention of problems frequently involves whole communities, although this is not always necessary. Prevention sometimes involves counseling, but not always. Because we lack a better term, we will use *preventive helping* to describe this whole process of helping people steer clear of potential problems before they arise.

Three Aims of Preventive Helping

In 1964 a psychiatrist named Gerald Caplan published a book titled *Principles of Preventive Psychiatry.* This book stimulated interest in the prevention of personal problems and led to what now has been called "the science of prevention." [1] It's a form of people helping that has three aims.

First, preventive helping attempts to *prevent problems from happening before they begin.* Sometimes called primary prevention, this involves anticipating problem situations before they arise and doing something at present to prevent unpleasant or undesirable things from occurring in the future. Sometimes primary prevention also involves taking action now that will increase the likelihood of something desirable happening in the future. [2]

Premarital counseling is an excellent example of this kind of prevention. While the couple is still anticipating marriage, both parties are alerted to potential problems between husbands and wives, are given instructions on how to prevent such problems from occurring, and learn what they can do to increase the likelihood of a good marriage.

Second, preventive helping attempts to *arrest or stop existing problems before they get worse.* This is called secondary prevention. It involves cutting the duration and the severity of a developing problem. When a church holds marriage-enrichment seminars for married couples, it is often engaging in secondary prevention. Problems that might have been developing are identified, dealt with, and sometimes stopped before they get worse.

It is difficult for an outsider to stop developing problems in the life of someone else. In their early stages, developing problems are often hidden—sometimes even from the person who has them—and for an outsider to intervene often is seen as meddling. People who are willing to admit that they have developing problems often do not want help because they feel capable of handling the situations themselves. Many times these people don't even want to change. Drinking or promiscuous sexual behavior might be pleasant at first, so people who engage in these activities often prefer to be left alone.

A third kind of preventive helping, known sometimes as *tertiary prevention,* tries to *reduce or eliminate the influences of previous problems.* Suppose, for example, that a former alcoholic, mental patient, or prisoner returns to his or her hometown and tries to get a job. Very often such a person encounters suspicion from others, criticism, prejudice, lack of acceptance, and a great deal of mistrust. This can be devastating to the person who is trying to move back into the community and return to a normal life. In situations like these, people helpers can work with both the individual and the community to make the transition smoother and to prevent a rejection that might lead the returning person to become so discouraged that he or she returns to the former ways of life.

Such discouragement came to a young man who attended a local high school. After a period of rebellion and conflict with teachers, he tried to make changes, "get his act together," and straighten out. His teachers and some classmates, however, continued to treat him like a burnout. Before long he quit trying to reform, went back to his previous burnout friends, and was kicked out of school a week before graduation.

Prevention in the Church and Community
How can we prevent kids from dropping out of school, grown men from gambling, young adults from being pro-

miscuous, or naive people from being lured into cults? How do we prevent AIDS, violence, teenage pregnancies, substance abuse, poor self-concepts, or bad family relations? These questions concern educators, politicians, pastors, professional counselors, and other people throughout the society. Researchers have tried education programs, teaching people new skills, mass media campaigns, peer discussion groups, and a number of other approaches to prevention, some of which work better than others. Until recently, however, many church leaders and Christian people helpers have been so busy solving existing problems that there has been little attention directed to prevention. But the Bible is filled with practical advice on how the church and individual believers can avoid problems and live more stable lives.

In many respects the entire church program contributes to the prevention of problems. Corporate worship, small group meetings, Bible study classes, seminars, and even Christian service can alert people to dangers and help them anticipate and avoid spiritual or psychological problems. This includes alerting people to the destructive tactics of Satan so that believers become like Paul, who was well aware of the devil's problem-producing schemes (2 Cor. 2:11).

Unlike some other forms of helping, prevention most often occurs outside the formal interview. When the pastor talks to a congregation about resisting the devil, when the youth director talks to the high school group about finding God's will in one's vocation, or when a pastor's wife talks to a women's group about being fulfilled as a woman, preventive helping is taking place. The same occurs when a campus worker talks with a college student about the Spirit-filled life or shows a group of students how to have a regular quiet time. The high school youth leader who chats over a Coke with some freshman about his mounting sexual urges is engaging in preventive helping, even though neither person may stop to realize that their conversation is a form of counseling focused on preventing future problems.

Prevention can help specific individuals avoid danger, stop problems that are developing, or readjust following the resolution of a previous problem, but preventive helpers can also work with groups, neighborhoods, or whole communities. Through government agencies or other means of intervention we can work to avoid or reduce harmful social conditions, such as economic depression, poverty, acts of crime and violence, or moral degeneration in the media. As a result, whole societies can avoid a potential stress and become more stable and less tense.

Most professional interest in the problem of prevention has focused on the whole community. In a field of study known as community psychology (or community psychiatry), professional counselors and others work in the streets or with government officials, service clubs, educational institutions, and the news media. By attempting to change society so that it is less stressful, these preventive people helpers assume that personal problems will be prevented, that existing difficulties will be reduced or even eliminated, and that the general level of mental health in a community will be improved.

The community psychology movement places great emphasis on schools, hospitals, and social service agencies but says very little about the role of the local church in the prevention of psychological disorders. In books on prevention or community psychology, the church or religion rarely get mentioned. This could be due to the anti-Christian bias of community psychologists, but it may be equally due to the church's failure to be more involved in the prevention of psychological problems.

Social historians sometimes overlook the role of the church

181

in bringing social change and in helping disadvantaged and underserved people. Significant but often unnoticed community counseling is done every day, especially by members of inner-city congregations, including those who lack the benefits of better-funded suburban churches. These church-based community people-helper programs are often more effective than their secular counterparts. When government and other programs lack funds for personnel, church members often serve without payment. When public programs falter because there is bureaucracy or a lack of commitment among workers, church members keep going because they reach out to others as an expression of their commitment to Jesus Christ. When there is nobody to give social support in the community, the church gives people access to caregivers who play an important role in "preventing mental breakdown and speeding recovery and reintegration into the community following breakdown." [3]

While a number of inner-city pastors and church members have been involved in community caring and preventive people helping, perhaps the earliest and most articulate leader in this field has been Howard Clinebell, who described the community mental health movement as "an exciting social revolution" that could have profound human significance and be "one of the most important social revolutions in the history of our country, perhaps of the world." [4] This may be overstated enthusiasm, but it stems from the conviction that if we can change the community, we can help people who are suffering from overt or hidden psychological problems. We can also do a great deal to prevent psychological difficulties from arising in people who are well adjusted today. In creative ways, Clinebell has shown how the church can play a significant role in changing society and in providing an environment where mental health will be stimulated.

This concept of prevention through social intervention has

been very popular among more liberal Christians. In one sense it is a new form of the old social gospel. Change the society, it argues, and we change the mental health of individuals. Most evangelical Christians would agree that it is desirable to change society and eliminate poverty, racial injustice, and other stress-producing conditions, but they would insist that the spiritual needs of individuals must also be met—by Jesus Christ—if there is to be lasting mental stability and the prevention of problems.

Preventive Helping and Discipleship

Nowhere is the issue of preventive counseling more clearly illustrated than in the area of discipleship. The disciple is being trained to cope with future stresses, deal with internal tensions, grow spiritually, and eventually move toward the goal of spiritual and psychological maturity. Mental health is sometimes defined as physical, intellectual, social, and spiritual maturity. Jesus is described in the Bible as a person who grew in stature (physically), in wisdom (intellectually), in favor with God (spiritually) and with human beings (socially). He was the epitome of good mental health, and he trained his disciples to meet their future problems in a healthy and creative manner.

Matthew 10 gives a superb example of the preventive counseling techniques that Jesus used. He was preparing to send the twelve disciples on a short training mission, but before they left, he prepared them for what they would encounter. By alerting them to potential problems, he enabled them to avoid difficulties that might otherwise have arisen. His methods for preventing future problems involved giving encouragement, warning the disciples about what was coming, telling them what to do if opposition came, giving them experience in facing problems, showing them how he handled stress, discussing with them the problems they encountered, and emphasizing that relaxation is a good way to build up resistance against future stress. We will consider each of these in turn.

Encouragement

The disciples may have been nervous and uncertain about their ability to carry on the work that Jesus had begun and expected them to continue. So he reassured them (Matt. 10:19, 26, 29-31), told them that their ministry was important (Matt. 10:40), and gave them the authority and power to face their future with confidence (Matt. 10:1; Luke 9:1). Perhaps this seems like a little thing, but the encouragement and prayerful support of another human being can be a valuable sustaining influence to help people as they face the future, try new ventures, change behavior, or otherwise deal with problems before they get worse.

Warning

The preparation that Jesus gave involved much more than encouragement. It warned of dangers to come. Jesus indicated that serving him might lead to disruption of families or to rejection from the people we love (Matt. 10:21-22, 34-36). Those words were not just scare tactics; they were a clear statement of the difficulties that Jesus' disciples could expect to face in the future.

Paul used a similar approach in Romans 16:19 when he wrote, "I want you to be wise about what is good, and innocent about what is evil" (v. 19). This gives no support to the idea that our warnings need to go into a lot of detail about the dangers that are ahead. Such detail can be harmful, especially when it scares people or stops them from moving ahead. We are to be "innocent about what is evil," yet alert enough to know what to avoid.

When we are warned that there are dangers ahead, we can

make efforts to steer clear of problems that might arise. The church has recognized this for centuries and has warned people about the dangers of involvement in compromising sex situations, dabbling in occult practices, maintaining self-centered attitudes in marriage, or uncritically accepting all that we read or hear in classrooms. Regrettably, these warnings aren't always received with gratitude or enthusiasm—especially when the warning comes to young people from those who are older. Even if the warning goes unheeded for the moment, however, it sometimes is remembered at a later time. Even this can be helpful. *I was warned about this,* a person might think when he or she encounters problems, *so I'm not surprised.* To be forewarned is often a help in avoiding problems or in stopping existing problems before they get worse.

Instruction

To warn a person that there is danger ahead may prevent a tragedy, but the warning is even more beneficial if we can help the person find some alternatives that are less dangerous. After Jesus warned the disciples, he did not leave them to fend for themselves. He told them specifically

- what to do when difficult situations arise (Matt. 10:6-8, 11-14, 23);
- what not to do in times of stress (Matt. 10:5b, 9-10); and
- how to handle feelings (Matt. 10:28).

This is a great guideline for a discipling program, but it also illustrates that part of the preventive helper's job is to educate people. To prevent problems, the helper can give instruction on topics such as how people can mature spiritu-

185

ally, improve their marriages, prepare for death, handle their impulses, meet frustrations, or cope with stress.

Sometimes instructive helping can create problems that might not be there otherwise. Consider, for example, the oft-quoted statement that "97 percent of all college men masturbate, and the other 3 percent are liars." What does this do to the freshman who has never thought about masturbating? Does it lead him into a problem that he might otherwise have avoided? This question has been raised by critics of sex education programs, who fear that a little knowledge can arouse curiosity and create problems that might otherwise be avoided.

While this kind of risk surely exists, sometimes there is greater risk in keeping silent. Young people are not as naive as their parents sometimes assume. Even to arouse doubt or curiosity might not be bad. It is better to have these occur while a mature helper is around than at some later time when the individual is alone and perhaps defenseless.

One other problem with giving instruction is something that concerns me whenever I teach a course, give a lecture, or write a book: Will any of this make a practical difference in people's lives? Most of us have had the experience of reading a book or hearing a sermon, concluding that "this is very helpful," and then promptly forgetting what we learned. The passive recipient of learning won't change nearly as much as the person who absorbs the new learning and acts on it immediately and in a practical way. Jesus followed this active-learning principle in preparing his disciples for the future.

Experience

Imagine what a football team would be like if its training consisted solely of encouragement, warnings of danger, and lectures on how to defeat the opposition. This is exactly how many churches, parents, and educational institutions attempt to prepare people to face the problems of life: with talk but with no practical training. Little wonder there is so much defeat!

In contrast to this, Jesus gave his disciples something to do. He sent them out for practical experience (Luke 9:2; 10:1) and guided them as they went. It is not easy to provide experience for people who are learning, and at times it isn't even ethical. Sometimes we can provide artificial learning situations like they do in theological schools, where students preach to each other, witness to each other, or counsel with each other before going out into the nearby community. But it is difficult, if not impossible, to give experience in, say, avoiding adultery or staying clear of the occult.

In situations where training is possible, we might begin by asking for suggestions about what to do and what not to do in the future. Together, the helper and helpee can evaluate these suggestions and try to think of some others, then discuss what actions to take and consider the dangers or potential for failure that are involved. As people try to take action to avoid problems, we can stick with them and perhaps even go with them as they move out to get experience. This, of course, is often what happens when people are trained to witness. After the instruction, and perhaps some practice, they go out like the followers of Jesus, two by two.

Jesus was more than a lecturer. In preparing his disciples to anticipate and cope with the stresses of their future ministry, he did not hide his involvement. Jesus rejoiced in their successes, helped them learn from their failures, prayed for them, and took obvious delight in their ministries (Luke 10:18-23).

Demonstration
Jesus also was a model to the disciples (Matt. 11:1). He showed them how to disciple others, how to cope with prob-

lems that existed, and how to avoid potentially dangerous situations. His example must have been very helpful when they faced problems alone in the future.

We all know of people whose lives have inspired others. This is another way to be a people helper: showing others how to live so they can have a model to follow when they face stress or other difficulties in the future.

Evaluation

Learning is always more effective when there is evaluation or feedback. Athletes learned this a long time ago, studies of learning support it, and Jesus demonstrated it. When the followers of Jesus returned after their training session, they gave a report and doubtless spent time evaluating their efforts (Luke 9:10; 10:17).

Relaxation

Jesus was a very busy man, but in the midst of all the demands, he took time to relax. In Luke 9:10 we read that after the disciples returned from their ministry and gave a report, Jesus took them with him, and they withdrew by themselves. Might this have been part of the training program? Maybe this was a lesson in preventive helping—showing that we should take time to rest and rejuvenate so we are better prepared to face future problems as they arise.

We live in a time when almost everyone is busy and the whole society moves quickly. Our bodies can take only so much of this pace and this change. If we fail to relax, we become much more subject to physical illness, tension, and difficulties in getting along with people. Even our spiritual lives suffer when we fail to rest periodically. At times we all need to be still while we get to know God better (Ps. 46:10).

We cannot be effective people helpers when we are rushed

and overwhelmed by the pressures of life. One of the best
ways we can help others to avoid problems is by encouraging
them to take the time to relax periodically—with a good
book, a game or hobby, a respected friend, or perhaps alone
by themselves. This is an essential part of preventive helping.
If we are rested, we face the problems of the future with
greater confidence and efficiency. The place to start is with
the helper who shows others how it is done.

Guidelines for Prevention

What can we conclude about the prevention of psychological and spiritual problems?

1. The best way to handle personal problems is to stop
them before they begin. When this fails we should intervene
early in a problem to stop it from getting worse.

2. The church is in a unique position to anticipate problems before they develop, to alert people to problems that
might come, to spot problems that could be developing,
and to intervene to prevent existing problems from getting
worse.

3. Christians should recognize that prevention of individual problems will require a number of attitudes on the part
of the helper. These include:

- *Foresight*—to see a potential or developing problem
  before it arises or gets worse;
- *Knowledge*—of how a stressful situation or environment can be changed, of where someone might be
  referred, or of what might be done about a developing
  problem situation;
- *Courage*—to get involved in trying to resolve newly
  developing problems, even though these are issues that
  we often ignore or overlook because we are too busy

189

with other things or are unwilling to give the appearance of meddling;

- *Tact*—in bringing up sensitive issues that people might not want to discuss and in not taking a holier-than-thou or a know-it-all attitude. People don't always like to be bothered about developing personal problems that are not yet serious;
- *Compassion*—which expresses so much concern and love for others that we are willing to risk being rejected if this will help prevent a problem; and
- *Planning*—so that dating, premarital, pre-middle-age or preretirement issues can be raised in a nonthreatening but forceful way, and so that marriage-enrichment seminars, spiritual-growth meetings, or sharing groups can be introduced in a way that will maximize the benefits to the participants and minimize the threat for the resistant people who most likely need the benefits.

4. Every aspect of the church's ministry—including preaching, teaching, evangelism, social gatherings, music, and service—should be planned in view of the present and future spiritual and psychological welfare of the participants.

5. Education is an important part of prevention. Christian people helpers must give serious consideration to ways we can educate people about such issues as how to have a better marriage; how to handle family conflicts; how to cope with stress; how to avoid backbiting, gossip, and other behaviors that create additional problems; how to be forgiving when people fall into sin; or how to get along with people. Jesus and the New Testament writers dealt with practical problems such as these, but contemporary Christians often ignore them. To do so is to let problems grow that otherwise might be prevented or stopped in the beginning.

Preventive People Helping and the Great Commission

The Great Commission is a beautiful example of preventive psychology. Jesus knew that living in this world was difficult, so he provided guidelines that would help us achieve maximum stability and benefit in our lives.

"Remember," he said in essence, "that I have all power and authority." This gives us *reassurance.*

"Go and make disciples." This gives us a *purpose* for living.

"Baptize and teach" gives us the *pattern* to follow.

"Remember the three persons of the Trinity." This creates *stability* and a reminder of the great God we serve.

"I am with you always, even to the end of the age" is a message that gives a sure *hope* for the present and future.

Paul was a man who had everything the world could give—status, education, riches, and self-confidence. But he became a disciple of Jesus Christ and a discipler of others. As such, he was able to endure all kinds of problems, and he helped others to do the same. In his second letter to Timothy, Paul gave some directions to his young disciple about preventing problems in himself and others. These directions are still relevant today:

> Do your best to present yourself to God as one approved, a workman who does not need to be ashamed and who correctly handles the word of truth. Avoid godless chatter, because those who indulge in it will become more and more ungodly. . . .
>
> Flee the evil desires of youth, and pursue righteousness, faith, love and peace, along with those who call on the Lord out of a pure heart. Don't have anything to do with foolish and stupid arguments, because you know they produce quarrels. And the Lord's servant must not quarrel; instead, he must be kind to everyone, able to teach, not resentful. Those who oppose him he must gently instruct, in the hope that

God will grant them repentance leading to a knowledge of the truth, and that they will come to their senses and escape from the trap of the devil, who has taken them captive to do his will (2 Tim. 2:15-16, 22-26).

Notes

1. The science of prevention is described in a somewhat technical article with nine authors, the first of whom is John D. Coie et al., "The Science of Prevention: A Conceptual Framework and Some Directions for a National Research Program," *American Psychologist* 48 (October 1993): 1013–22. See also Gerald Caplan, *Principles of Preventive Psychology* (New York: Basic Books, 1964).

2. George W. Albee and Kimberly D. Ryan-Finn, "An Overview of Primary Prevention," *Journal of Counseling and Development,* 72 (November/December, 1993): 115–23.

3. Rodger K. Bufford and Trudi Bratten Johnston, "The Church and Community Mental Health: Unrealized Potential," *Journal of Psychology and Theology* 10 (winter 1982): 355–62.

4. Howard J. Clinebell Jr., ed., *Community Mental Health: The Role of Church and Temple* (Nashville: Abingdon, 1970), 11. See also Kenneth I. Pargament, Kenneth I. Maton, and Robert E. Hess, eds., *Religion and Prevention in Mental Health: Research, Vision, and Action* (New York: Haworth Press, 1992).

CHAPTER TWELVE

Helping Yourself

SOME TIME AGO I was sitting in a restaurant where, to put it mildly, the service was less than efficient. After a long wait for our coffee, I caught the waiter's attention and asked (politely, I thought) if he could fill my cup. His reply was curt and to the point: "I'll get to you when I can, sir! Can't you see that I have people to wait on?"

A friend who was sitting at the table made a poignant reply: "What does he mean: He has people to wait on? Doesn't he know that I'm a people, too!"

Perhaps you have thought something similar as you have been reading the previous pages. We have focused mostly on how we can help others, but we need to remember that the helper is "a people, too." There are times when we who are help givers need to receive a little help for ourselves. It isn't easy for counselors to admit that sometimes we are the ones who need encouragement, support, insight, guidance, and challenges from other counselors. At times we also must think of ways to help ourselves.

There is debate among professional counselors about the extent to which helpers can help themselves, especially when they are facing psychological problems. We value Christian counseling, but even people helpers can be reluctant to share burdens with another person. Often there is unwillingness to admit that we who are the helpers of others might need help for ourselves. Instead, we follow the lead of many of our helpees and turn to a self-help book or tape.

The Self-Help Business

A reporter from the *Los Angeles Times* estimates that more than two thousand self-help books are published every year.[1] These cover almost every topic imaginable, are hyped by enthusiastic publishers and authors, often are written by and for Christians, and promise to help readers deal on their own with spiritual, behavioral, relational, and emotional problems. The production and sale of self-help materials has been called a big business that is "growing beyond imagination." Bookstores, shopping malls, direct-mail catalogs, and even church libraries overflow with do-it-yourself books, self-help audio cassettes, video tapes, and computer self-change programs. These materials are marketed with bold claims and are aimed at the millions of needy people who want to find help in dealing with their problems and insecurities.

Critics note that many books and tapes are produced and marketed in ways that appear to have two primary goals: to make sales and to enhance the reputations of their authors. Often these materials make claims that are pure speculation. The authors and publishers promise that the materials will bring change, but nobody has carefully tested whether or not this is true. For example, a book on handling fears carried these words on the cover: "In as little as six to eight weeks, without the expense of professional counseling, and in the privacy of your own home, you can learn to master those situations that now make you nervous or afraid."[2] There was nothing to back up this claim other than these words on the book cover. We can only guess what happens to people who read the book and don't change in accordance with the promised hype. Some might sink deeper into their problems and conclude that their situations are hopeless. Probably many others return to the bookstore looking for a different book.

Despite these weaknesses, many self-help books and other materials give genuinely helpful guidance to people who don't know where else to turn, don't have a counselor who is available, are embarrassed to admit their problems, or cannot afford professional help. Others are not looking for relief from serious problems but instead want to increase their knowledge and find ways to improve themselves and build better relationships. One survey of psychologists found that 90 percent thought self-help books could be helpful, and 60 percent encouraged their clients to read them.[3] Many Christian counselors recommend books to their helpees,[4] and nonprofessional people helpers can do the same.

How do we distinguish the good books from rest? Look at the credentials of the person who has written the book or produced the materials. See if there are endorsements. Are these from people whose opinion you respect and trust? Ask if there is any research to support what the author is saying. If the author, speaker, or publisher makes bold claims, try to answer the question, How do we know that this is true? In time you will find that some publishers and some authors are more trustworthy than others, but be cautious about believing everything you read in an advertisement, see in print, or hear on a tape. Like everybody else, the people who produce self-help materials are fallible human beings. Most have good intentions, but their conclusions are not always as helpful as they might claim.

Despite these cautions, we—like those we seek to help—can benefit from books, tapes, seminars, mutual-aid support groups, or other resources that offer counsel, support, and accountability. Many of these resources offer practical, helpful suggestions, and many encourage us to keep looking at ourselves.

Look at Yourself

In the medical world, diagnosis of a problem usually precedes treatment, and the same can be true in helping ourselves (and others). If we can find out what's wrong and what needs to be changed, we are well on the way to doing something about our problems.

Of course, this is a lot easier said than done. It is difficult to examine our own life with much objectivity, and even after we get some idea of what is wrong and what needs to be done, change is not always easy. Nevertheless, this self-examination is important in self-help, and it can take place on three levels.

Looking at ourselves in the light of Scripture
Psalm 119 begins with some very helpful advice:

> Blessed are they whose ways are blameless, who walk according to the law of the Lord. . . . How can a young man keep his way pure? By living it according to your Word. (vv. 1, 9)

In our daily reading of the Bible we need to be testing our behavior, attitudes, thinking, and feelings against the divine Word of God. God knows our inner psychic problems and struggles better than we do. He can help us to know ourselves better, and his Holy Spirit will assist us as we change (Ps. 139). Before reading the Bible, we should ask God to teach us the specific things we need to know about him and about ourselves.

Looking at ourselves by self-evaluation

Second, we can look at ourselves in terms of our own perceived strengths and weaknesses. When I taught seminary courses in counseling, each student was required to write an autobiography that included a listing of his or her strengths and weaknesses, goals and life priorities, present problems and plans for changing in ways that would make things better. Sometimes this was a difficult assignment, but almost always it was a valuable exercise because it forced each student to take an honest self-evaluation. Something similar can be helpful for all of us, especially if our self-examinations are ongoing.

Looking at ourselves as others see us

These self-analyses can be even more helpful if we can share them with somebody else. Sharing is a third way of knowing ourselves. It is an idea that all counselors accept but that many of us fail to put into practice, in part because it can be threatening to see ourselves as others see us.

Families and close friends often know us better than we know ourselves, and at times their evaluations can be both painful and revealing. Near the end of her long life, my mother developed some attitudes that bothered me. I was able to overlook them, especially because I valued our relationship and didn't think that much could be gained by even gently confronting my mother about her ways of thinking. One day, however, I was discussing this with one of my daughters. "Don't let me ever get like Grandma in this respect," I suggested, almost in passing.

"Dad," my daughter replied, "you already are like Grandma." Before I could get defensive, my daughter confessed (with a twinkle in her eye) that she was seeing some of the same attitudes in herself. We agreed to help one another stop some of our emerging ways of thinking.

Often it is helpful to take a more direct approach to seeing ourselves as others see us. Each of us can benefit from sharing struggles, insecurities, dreams, and other personal issues with some other person who is willing to listen and give feedback. It could be argued that we cannot really know ourselves until we have disclosed ourselves to at least one other significant person. This sharing can be overdone, of course. Most of us know people who talk incessantly about themselves and their struggles so that everybody nearby hears the details, often over and over, and everybody except the speaker is bored. In contrast are those who keep so much to themselves that they are not known by anybody. A more balanced and healthy alternative is to share openly with a spouse or with close friends who lovingly can give honest feedback, encouragement, and guidance when it is needed.

Learn to Accept Yourself

Every one of us has a self-concept, a picture of who we are and what we are like. If you think, *I'm a good Christian, I'm a poor housekeeper, I'm too fat,* or *I'm God's gift to women,* these are all a part of your self-concept or self-image.

The best way to get a clear picture of this is to write a list of the adjectives that describe you. The list may include your physical features (like good-looking, balding, or big nose), your personality characteristics (such as friendly, impatient, or outgoing), your abilities and beliefs ("I am a woman who believes in God"), your moral values ("I am a person who is opposed to abortion"), and the various roles that you fulfill (such as husband, father, son, deacon, businessman, Boy Scout leader, etc.). In looking over the list you will find that some of the things listed are desirable (such as being a friendly person), while others are less desirable (for example, being lazy). Some parts of your self-image are likely to be held firmly, but you may be less sure about other parts.

Self-image is important because it determines a lot of our behavior. If a woman sees herself as being a capable business person, for example, she will operate much differently than the person who believes she has no business sense. The college professor who recognizes that he is a good teacher but a less capable researcher will show behavior in line with this self-perception. Others may disagree with our self-analyses, but most often we behave, think, and even feel in accordance with the self-concepts that each of us has built up over years of learning.

Many Christians have developed the attitude that committed believers should have a poor self-image, that it is a mark of spiritual maturity for Christians to be always putting themselves down. Because of this attitude many of our lives are miserable, and we go around boasting about how no good we are.

We need to recognize that while we were and are sinners, absolutely incapable of bringing about our own salvation, we are also human beings created in the image of God. In fact, God valued us so much that he sent his Son to pay the penalty for our sin through his own death. We are not forced to submit our life to this Christ—God allows us to have some free choice—but when we do submit, we become new creatures. We are filled with the Holy Spirit, given special spiritual gifts, and accorded the privilege of serving the sovereign Lord of the universe. God now considers us to be his own sons and daughters (Rom. 8:15; Gal. 4:4-7; Eph. 5:1), whom he knows and cares for personally. It is true, of course, that none of this came because we are worthy of special treatment. It came solely because of the goodness and mercy of God.

This awareness should change one's self-image drastically. We are valuable people, children of the King, not because of our actions or lifestyles, but because of what he has done. We don't deny our abilities or successes. We accept them as coming from God, acknowledge them with gratitude, and develop a positive self-image based on what God has done and is doing in our life.

Be a Disciple

It is not easy to be honest in looking at ourself or in sharing with another person. But it can be hard, as well, to be honest with God.

When he created the human race, God placed us in a superb environment and clearly intended that human beings should have a close and intimate relationship with their Creator. Unwilling to make us robots, God gave us a will and with it the freedom to turn against him. This is what happened, first in the Garden of Eden and later in the lives of Adam and Eve's descendants.

The Bible uses an unpopular word to describe human rebellion. It is called *sin,* and it is part of us all (Rom. 3:10-12, 23). Sin cuts us off from God, but it does even more than this. It lies at the root of all our problems. For this reason, sooner or later we must face the fact of sin if we are to help people, including ourself. We must confess our own sin and, through prayer, invite Jesus Christ to become Lord of our life (Rom. 10:9; 1 John 1:9). By doing this, we are assured of eternal life in heaven and a full, abundant life here on earth (John 3:16; 10:10).

The Bible says nothing about salvation by good works, baptism, church membership, or anything else. Salvation is a gift from God that we may accept, reject, or ignore, but never earn (Rom. 6:23; Eph. 2:8-9).

When a person makes this commitment to Jesus Christ, his or her immediate problems *may* disappear suddenly, but often they stay the same, and sometimes they get worse. Even so, in the midst of our problems we have peace with God (Rom. 5:1) and a new source of power for coping with life and maintaining mental stability (2 Tim. 1:7). To become a disciple of Jesus Christ is an important part of people helping because it lets us commit our problems to an almighty and wise God who is touched by our difficulties and willing to do something about them (1 Pet. 5:7).

I have a colleague who tells his helpees, "I don't know what to do about your problem, but I have a Friend who does!" This is an encouraging truth, especially in times of stress. This divine Friend can help both helpers and helpees.

Walk in the Spirit

A lot of people commit their lives to Christ but don't seem to grow spiritually. They stay "babes in Christ" throughout their lives, and because of this immaturity, they have trouble understanding the Bible, getting along with people, and dealing with an exploding temper or with inner attitudes like jealousy (1 Cor. 3:1-3). To grow as Christians we need to be imitators of Christ.

Ephesians 5 tells what this means. To be an imitator of Christ means that our lifestyle is to be characterized by love (Eph. 5:2), moral purity (vv. 3-7), behavior that is pleasing to God (vv. 8-14), wisdom (vv. 15-17), and "being filled with the Spirit," (v. 18). In Galatians 5:16, Paul calls this "walking in the Spirit," and it is the secret of Christian growth.

Before the Crucifixion, Jesus promised that the Holy Spirit would come as a comforter-teacher, and the disciples experienced the Spirit's power on the Day of Pentecost (Acts 2). Most Christians believe that when we commit ourselves to Christ, the Holy Spirit comes to live inside us. He never leaves, but he can be "quenched" or put down (1 Cor. 6:19; 1 Thess. 5:19).

Instead of this, Christians are to "walk in the Spirit" every day. This involves frequently examining ourselves and confessing sin, submitting ourselves completely to God, and asking the Holy Spirit to fill us (Luke 11:13; Rom. 6:11-13; 1 John 1:9). Ephesians 5:18 adds that we should keep on being filled with the Spirit, letting him control our lives daily. The results may not seem outwardly spectacular, but we soon discover (and so do others) that the fruit of the Spirit is growing in our life. This fruit is not like apples and oranges. Instead, it includes love, joy, peace, patience, kindness, goodness, faithfulness, gentleness, and self-control (Gal. 5:22-23).

All of this does not come as the result of some self-help formula. It is a personality transformation that comes because we have made the decision to walk in the Spirit and let him control our life and emotions.

Three circles

In chapter 2 we suggested that thinking, feeling, and actions are all important in the individual's life. What distinguishes Christians who are walking in the Spirit from other people is the center around which their lives revolve. For the nonbeliever it is the self.

In the nongrowing Christian, Christ has entered his or her life but has been pushed to the sidelines, so that thinking, feeling, and behavior are still pretty much self-centered and self-directed.

When we walk in the Spirit, however, Christ has come to the center of our life, and he controls all three parts through the Holy Spirit. Notice that we do not lose our unique personalities so that the self is eliminated. Our self-interests are submitted to Christ, but he works out through the self to influence our thoughts, feelings, and actions. When this happens, we begin to grow as Christians. This should be a prime goal for disciples and disciplers, including ourself.

Growth in maturity

The Christian life is not a straitjacket of rules and regulations; it is a life that gives us freedom to grow. But like any growing organism, the Christian grows faster when he or she follows a few rules for good health.

In Romans 8:29 we read that God wants his followers to be made into the image of his Son. The goal of our life should be to be like Jesus. This means that we should get to know him as intimately as possible. We do this by Bible study and frequent contact with him through prayer. Every Christian knows this, but so often we find excuses to avoid the intake of spiritual food that is so essential for spiritual growth and development.

In addition to this feeding, exercise is vital. Have you ever noticed how often the Bible ties together *what God does for us* with *what we do for others?* The Lord's Prayer is a good example: "Forgive us our debts, as we also have forgiven our debtors. . . . For if you forgive men when they sin against you, your heavenly Father will also forgive you. But if you do not forgive men their sins, your Father will not forgive your sins" (Matt. 6:12-15).

In the Sermon on the Mount the principle is repeated: "Blessed are the merciful, for they will be shown mercy" (Matt. 5:7). "For in the same way you judge others, you will be judged, and with the measure you use, it will be measured to you" (Matt. 7:2). In writing to the Philippians, Paul assures his readers that his "God shall supply all your needs" (Phil. 4:19), but he has just noted that the Philippians had been very generous in supplying Paul's own needs. James warns that "judgment without mercy will be shown to anyone who has not been merciful" (James 2:13).

There appears to be a principle here that applies to people helpers when we want forgiveness, fair treatment, material things, love, help, attention, or any number of other things. The best place to start receiving is by giving to others. By helping someone else, we grow in Christian maturity, we help ourselves in the process, and our needs are met as we provide for others.

Discover and Develop Your Spiritual Gifts

In an earlier chapter we noted that every believer has a spiritual gift or gifts. By discovering these gifts and developing them we find our real purpose in life, and each of us has the satisfaction of making a unique contribution to the body of Christ.

Although the Bible doesn't give us an exact formula for finding our spiritual gifts, we can be sure that the same God who tells us we have gifts will help us uncover what they are. You can begin by asking yourself questions such as the following:

- What special abilities do others see in me?
- What am I most often asked to do, and what am I never asked to do?
- What do I enjoy doing? (God is not a killjoy; he wants us to be happy in the way we serve him.)
- In what am I most successful? (This may require a little trial and error.)

- Do these successful activities enrich or profit others? Do they build up the body of Christ?

Gifts often emerge clearly, but even before we have a complete knowledge of our gifts, we can start serving. By trial and error we soon discover those gifts that are given to us by God and are useful for helping the whole body of Christ.

Getting Help by Shifting Burdens

I like to handle things by myself. Sometimes I face difficulties by withdrawing or getting depressed, but in general I feel better when I am in control of a situation and can do something about it. It is easy for me to share this because it seems that most people are the same—at least in countries where individualism and technology are both highly valued.

But the Scriptures give us a different message. In the Old and New Testaments we are told to cast our burdens on the Lord (Ps. 55:22; 1 Pet. 5:7). Jesus also emphasized this (Matt. 6:25; 11:28-29), but many Christians are slow to get the message. We either carry all our cares on our own shoulders, or we give them to God in prayer and then take them back.

Paul had this problem. He had a "thorn in the flesh" that kept him worrying. One day he realized that God knew all about this burden, so Paul let him handle the situation and relaxed (2 Cor. 12:7-10). In contrast, we read in the Old Testament that Jacob tried to run his own life. He engaged in intellectual scheming and even deception to get his way. Then he went to stay with Laban and met someone who was equally crafty. Only as he wrestled with God was Jacob able to submit and hand his whole life over to the Lord.

The North American spirit of independence and rugged individualism gets many of us into a similar bind. When there are financial difficulties, problems in dealing with a wayward child, the need to find a new place to live, or the desire to build a career or expand a ministry, we start scheming to make it all happen. Sometimes we succeed and sometimes we fail, but often we carry a burden that shouldn't be ours to bear.

This is not a plea for inactivity and a lack of foresight; it is a reminder that our sovereign God knows all about our life. We need to develop the practice of casting our burdens on him and trusting him to work out solutions instead of trying to do everything ourselves. This is an important step in self-help: to "cease striving" and know that he is the exalted God (Ps. 46:10).

Join a Group and Do Something Positive

Since the beginning of Alcoholics Anonymous over half a century ago, hundreds of thousands have been part of a successful rehabilitation program in which people with a drinking problem have helped one another. Subsequently, great numbers of self-help, mutual-aid, support, and recovery groups have met consistently and been helpful to people struggling with almost every problem imaginable. These groups foster interpersonal sharing, caring, and self-disclosure, and this, in turn, often leads to high levels of intimacy, support, feelings of acceptance and belonging, commitment, and accountability.

Sometimes activity and involvement with others can be the best types of therapy. Even so, many of us probably are guilty of what has been called the *gold rush syndrome.* In gold rush days the prospector didn't dare stop to help another man who might be having trouble. To do so was to lose time, and then someone else, maybe even the man who was helped, might beat out the helper in finding the best claim. The result was a highly individualized, self-centered, private existence. Like the men who passed by the wounded traveler before the Good Samaritan came along, we hurry on through life, engrossed in our own little worlds and perhaps bearing our own burdens. We push toward our own goals and fail to realize that to help another person has great therapeutic value for the help giver. This isn't the only solution to our problems, but when we help somebody else, we often get the greatest benefit ourselves.

Find a Counselor

Surely one of the best ways to help ourselves is to find someone who can help us get a better perspective on life and cope with our problems. Many of us are reluctant to do this. It seems to imply that we are weak and incapable of solving our own problems. In reality, however, to find a helper and admit our weakness is really a sign of strength (2 Cor. 12:10). It means that we have faced the problem squarely and decided to find another person whose expertise and objectivity can assist us, in the same way that we might at some time give help in return.

Receiving help is always difficult. It can make us feel weak or inferior, and it contradicts the rugged individualism that we have come to value so highly. In reality we are all weak and in need of each other. To get the help we need makes a lot more sense than sitting around feeling sorry for ourselves and struggling (with repeated failures) to get on top of a situation that we may not fully understand or control. One of the factors that makes for growth in maturity is to accept the help and ministry of other Christians and counselors.

A Final Word

In all of our helping, whether we try to help ourselves or others, let us never lose sight of our goal. The Great Commission instructs, indeed commands, every Christian to witness and make disciples. Given power by Christ, we are to be his instruments in changing lives.

The change starts with us as individuals. Are you really a follower of Christ? Are you growing as a disciple? Are you touching others with the message of the gospel? Are you reaching out to assist others in the body of Christ as they grow to Christian maturity? Are you, like Paul, contributing to the training of others (including your family members) so that they in turn can be disciples and disciplers? If the answer to any of these questions is no, then you need to make changes in your own life. If you can answer yes, you already are a people helper, whether you realize it or not.

Notes

1. Gerald M. Rosen, "Self-Help or Hype? Comments on Psychology's Failure to Advance Self-Care," *Professional Psychology: Research and Practice* 24 (August 1993): 340–45. Some of the material in this section of the book is adapted from the Rosen article.
2. Gerald M. Rosen, *Don't Be Afraid* (Englewood Cliffs, N.J.: Prentice Hall, 1976).
3. Cited by Albert Ellis, "The Advantages and Disadvantages of Self-Help Therapy Materials," *Professional Psychology: Research and Practice* 24 (August 1993): 335–39.
4. M. Atwater and D. Smith, "Christian Therapists' Utilization of Bibliotherapeutic Resources," *Journal of Psychology and Theology* 10 (1982): 230–35.

People Helper
Growth Exercises
For Personal Reflection and Group Interaction

CHAPTER ONE The Heart of People Helping

1. What makes you interested in being a people helper? On a sheet of paper list your reasons. Be extremely honest, and do not simply list the politically correct answers. Discuss some of these with your group.
2. People helping is mentioned often in the Bible. Look up each of the following references and consider how God helps people: Psalm 46:1; Proverbs 3:5-6; Isaiah 40:31; Philippians 4:19; Hebrews 4:16; 13:6. Now look up the following and jot down how God uses people to help others: Matthew 10:8; Romans 12:15, 20; Galatians 6:2; 1 John 3:17.
3. "People helping is everybody's business." What do you think about this statement by the author? What support does the Bible give for this position? (Consider Matt. 10:8; Rom. 12:15, 20; Gal. 6:2; 1 John 3:17.)
4. If being a disciple of Jesus Christ is the basic requirement

for Christian people helpers, then it is important to take a close look at our commitment to personally growing as a follower of Jesus before embarking on the people-helping journey. How is Jesus impacting your values, goals, priorities, and purposes in life right now? Do you see any areas needing improvement? If so, how do you plan to make the necessary positive changes? Share some of these with the group.

5. The author lists three primary characteristics of being a disciple: obedience, love, and fruitfulness. If Jesus were to sit down next to you as your counselor, what would he say to you about these three areas of your life?

6. Being a disciple of Jesus Christ has a definite cost. What sacrifices or costs do you anticipate paying as you seek to seriously follow Jesus Christ and help others with their concerns and struggles? Discuss these with the group.

7. For a moment imagine yourself as someone seeking help. How would you want to be treated? What would you hope to get out of meeting with a people helper?

CHAPTER TWO The Basics of People Helping

1. If being a disciple of Jesus Christ is a basic requirement for Christian people helpers, the place to start helping is with a look at yourself. Have you invited Jesus Christ to be Lord and Savior of your life (John 3:16; Rom. 10:9)? Are you seeking to turn away from sin and confessing sin when it does occur (1 John 1:9; 2:1)? Are you regularly reading the Bible, spending time in prayer, and worshiping with other believers (1 Thess. 5:17; 2 Tim. 3:14-17; Heb. 10:25)? If you answered no to any of these questions, how do you plan to change?

2. People-Helper Principle No. 1 states that the personality,

values, attitudes, and beliefs of the helper are of primary importance. What personal issues and concerns are you struggling with right now? List them and again be honest—God already knows!

3. In looking over your list for question 2, what struggles would you be willing to share in a counseling role-play with another group member? Break up into pairs, and role-play with one person acting as the people helper and the other as the helpee. Switch roles. After finishing, discuss with your partner the role play. What was helpful and not so helpful? How could it have been better?

4. Do you think the helping skills of empathy, warmth, and genuineness can be learned? On a scale of 1 to 10, rate yourself on each of these skills. What practical steps can you take to improve your rating in any one of these areas? Discuss this in your group.

5. People-Helper Principle No. 2 states that the helpee's attitudes, expectations, and desires are important determinants of effective helping. What could you do to help motivate a helpee who does not expect to change or who is not enthusiastic about being helped?

6. People-Helper Principle No. 3 emphasizes the importance of the relationship in the helping process. How can we work on developing good rapport with our helpees? How would your approach to a teenager struggling with his or her sexuality differ from your approach to a bedridden nursing-home patient?

7. What is your reaction to the author's claim that thoughts, feelings, and behavior are all important considerations in the helping process? In which of these areas are you most comfortable operating? In which are you least comfortable? How can you increase your comfort level in your weaker areas?

CHAPTER THREE   The Techniques of People Helping

1. What did Jesus teach about helping people? Look at the following examples and list some conclusions: Mark 10:13-29; Luke 10:25-37; 24:13-35; John 8:2-11. Can you think of other examples?

2. In order to get a sense of the importance of attending skills, pair up with someone in your group. One of you will disclose an item of personal interest, while the other attempts to violate all the rules of good attending (poor eye contact, poor listening, etc.). Switch roles after a few minutes. After finishing, discuss how it felt when you were not attended to by your partner. What kind of impact would the lack of attending have on someone seeking help from you?

3. The skill of basic empathy is one way in which helpers communicate that they are truly listening to helpees. James 1:19 also emphasizes the importance of listening. What makes listening difficult for you? What can you do to try and improve your listening skills? How do you feel when someone is really listening to you?

4. In order to practice listening for all three areas of concern in helping (thoughts, feelings, behaviors), break up into groups of three. Role-play a typical counseling situation (e.g., mom with troubled teenager, father with work difficulties, etc.) where one will act as the helpee, one as the helper, and one as the observer. Using empathic listening skills, communicate your understanding of the helpee in all three areas. After five minutes, allow the observer and helpee to give the helper feedback on his or her performance. Switch roles and repeat.

5. Think about your relationships with other people. Do you tend to be quick to confront or hesitant to confront others? How should we confront others (see Matt. 7:1; Gal. 6:1)? If you are too quick to confront, what steps can you take to

become more gentle? If you find confrontation difficult, what can you do to become more assertive in confronting others?

6. How are people helping and discipleship related? What implications does the discipling process have on people helping? Practically, how will this impact your people helping?

CHAPTER FOUR The Direction of People Helping

1. Can you think of any mentoring relationships in the Bible? What characterized these relationships, and how could this apply to you? Look at Ruth 1. Read 2 Timothy 2:2, and consider the relationship between Paul and Timothy (see 1 Cor. 4:17; Phil. 2:22; 1 Tim. 1:18; 2 Tim. 1:1-14).

2. Effective listening, like playing an instrument, takes practice. Break up into groups of three (helper, helpee, observer), and role-play a counseling situation. Remember not to go beyond what the helpee says; simply reflect back in your own words the helpee's thoughts, feelings, and behaviors.

3. Discuss the author's statement: "There needs to be a long period of listening, understanding, and exploration before we start moving into solutions." What dangers are involved in giving advice or pressuring action too quickly? In thinking about your past helping relationships, do you tend to move too rapidly or too slowly toward implementing solutions? What practical steps can you take to help you slow down (or speed up) the process of moving toward suggesting solutions?

4. Step 3 of the model involves *exploring alternatives* that could be used to implement changes in a helpee's life. As a group, brainstorm possible action strategies for helpees in difficult situations (e.g., college student struggling with dating, single mom attempting to balance work and kids, man wrestling with addiction to pornography, etc.). Be realistic and creative!

5. Break up into groups of three, and choose one of the problem situations you discussed in question 4. Then formulate the best action plan. It is important to be specific and detailed in the implementation of the plan, so work together to flesh out how the helpee could make these changes in his or her daily life. As a helper, what can you do to help motivate the helpee to follow through on the plan?

6. The needs of the world around us can be overwhelming, but we can make a difference one person at a time. Think about people in your life right now. Is there anyone who could use your help or to whom you could be a mentor? Brainstorm strategies of how you can impact this person (Step 3), and formulate a specific plan (Step 5) to put your strategy into action. Begin the adventure of people helping with this plan!

CHAPTER FIVE   Paraprofessional People Helping

1. The Bible is filled with references about helping our brothers and sisters in Christ. In the following verses look for some practical guidelines for friend-to-friend helping: Zechariah 7:9; Matthew 18:15; Luke 17:3-4; Romans 14:10-13; 1 Corinthians 8:9-13; Galatians 6:1; James 1:19; 2:1-5; 5:19-20; 1 John 2:9-10. What does Galatians 1:10 suggest about restricting our helping to fellow believers?

2. Practice your effective listening skills with another role play of a counseling situation. In groups of three (helper, helpee, observer) continue to work on listening for thoughts, feelings, and behaviors. Make sure to take time to get feedback from the helpee and observer after you have completed the role play. Ask what you did well and what could be improved. Switch roles with the other group members, and do this exercise again if you have time.

3. Do you think you have a special gift of people helping?

What evidence would indicate the presence of this gift in a believer's life? Can someone still be a people helper even if he or she does not feel especially gifted?

4. Richard Foster states that money, sex, and power are three hooks that can leave us snared in sin's trap. Break up into groups of three, and discuss what dangers you personally need to be most careful to avoid. (Examples include overactive curiosity, sexual stimulation, confidence leaks, imbalanced spiritual emphasis). What practical steps can you take to prevent problems like these in the future?

5. In Table 5-1 the author lists eight characteristics for people helping. On a scale of 1 to 10, rate yourself on each of these characteristics. What does this indicate about the suitability of your becoming a people helper? How can you work to improve areas in which you have low scores? Share this with other group members if you feel comfortable in doing so.

CHAPTER SIX Stress and People Helping

1. Read Colossians 3:1-17. What does this portion of Scripture teach about the mind (v. 2); immorality and greed (vv. 5-7); anger, criticism, and lying (vv. 8-10); compassion, patience, forgiveness, love, and peace (vv. 12-15); Bible study and worship (v. 16); and daily living (v. 17)? In what ways does Colossians 3:1-17 help you deal with stress? How does Philippians 4:4-9 help? Be specific.

2. Once again, break up into groups of three, and have the helpee disclose how stress is having an impact on his or her life. Use active listening and empathy to respond both to the positives and negatives shared by the helpee. Give the observer feedback, and then switch roles.

3. Given the fact that stress is an undeniable aspect of modern

life, how can a knowledge of the causes and responses to stress make us better people helpers?

4. Break up into groups of four and discuss the following situation. A man in his midthirties comes to you for help. He is a father with two small children (eight and five) who lost his wife in a car accident one year ago. What types of stress is he likely experiencing? What can you do as a people helper to help him manage these stresses?

5. Think about the group of people with whom you are most likely to work as a helper. What unique stresses do they face? What can you do to help them face these stresses in their lives?

6. Encouragement is a powerful tool that can lift the spirits of those who are feeling burdened by the weight of the world. In your group discuss some practical ways in which you can encourage others. How can clichés that sound encouraging on the surface actually be counterproductive (e.g., "Just trust Jesus!" or "Just pray it through!")?

7. Perform an act of senseless kindness this week, and share what you did with the group next session.

CHAPTER SEVEN Helping in a Crisis

1. The Bible mentions a number of crisis situations, including Moses and the Israelites fleeing from Pharaoh's army, Jonah in the fish's belly, and Daniel in the den of lions. Second Corinthians 11:23-28 summarizes some of the crises of the apostle Paul. John 11:1-44 records another crisis. Of course we cannot raise anybody from the dead, but what can we learn about crisis counseling from this chapter?

2. Break up into groups of three (helper, helpee, observer) and role-play a crisis situation (such as a spouse who has just lost his or her partner, or a person who has experienced the

unexpected layoff of the primary wage earner in the family).
Use the basic skills of active listening and of empathy,
keeping in mind the unique features of crisis helping.

3. The author distinguishes between two major types of crises:
developmental and accidental. How would your helping
differ for each category of crisis? How would it be similar?

4. Think back on a time of personal crisis in your life. What
was done that was helpful to you? What was not beneficial?
What else could have been done for you?

5. Experiencing a crisis can generate strong emotions. How
comfortable are you with intense expression of anger, grief,
despair, etc.?

6. Helping in a crisis often involves being more directive and
practical than usual. Make a list of crisis situations that could
happen to people in your church. As a people helper, what
practical help could you give in each of these crisis situations?

7. Think about your circle of friends and acquaintances. Is
there anyone experiencing a developmental or accidental
crisis? What are some ways in which you could help? Determine to do something this week for the person in crisis.

CHAPTER EIGHT Helping When People Are Desperate

1. In the Old Testament, Job was a man who experienced a
number of crises one after another. (Read the first two
chapters of Job.) There is no evidence that he considered
suicide, but he did question the value of living. How did
Job's comforters help in the last three verses of chapter 2?
Later they became more of a hindrance than a help. Look at
the following verses, and see how Job reacts and how God
responds: Job 19:1-3; 32:3; 42:7. What does this teach you
about helping people in deep need?

2. The thought of helping a suicidal person can be frightening

for a new people helper. In the group discuss what concerns you have about helping in a suicidal situation.

3. In groups of three, role-play a situation in which the helpee is suicidal. What clues are important to notice? How can you evaluate the seriousness of the situation?

4. Referral is often a wise decision for people helpers who are faced with a suicidal helpee. What resources are available in your community? What steps would you take in making a referral?

5. Self-knowledge is an essential attribute in a people helper. What symptoms or problems in a helpee would make you uncomfortable or eager to refer the helpee? In general, what type of problems should be referred?

6. Discuss how you would handle a suicidal helpee who refuses to be referred. What options are available if there are no professional counselors in your community?

7. How would you respond to one of the contemporary critics of psychology who believes that we should never refer Christian helpees to professional counselors?

8. A woman in your congregation approaches you after the evening prayer service and says, "The irgin Mary was talking to me again tonight, and she keeps telling me to divorce my husband!" What do you do?

CHAPTER NINE Helping on the Telephone

1. For obvious reasons, the Bible never refers to helping people by talking with them on the telephone. But the Scriptures have many examples of helping people from a distance. Perhaps the best examples are found in the New Testament epistles, but look at Matthew 11:1-5. Who needed the help? What was the problem? How did Jesus help? What can we learn from this example?

2. What are some unique challenges of helping over the telephone? How can we overcome some of these obstacles?

3. Break up into pairs, turn back to back (so you can't see one another), and role-play a crisis-helping situation that you are handling by phone. How did your helping differ when you had no nonverbal awareness? What skills and techniques become more important in this situation?

4. Look over the list of "Games People Helpers Play." Which ones do you find yourself playing periodically? What can you do to end the games?

5. What telephone services are available to help people in your community? Make a list, and keep it for future reference.

6. Assume that an acquaintance calls, and you can tell from this person's tone of voice that he or she is obviously upset. However, the conversation remains superficial (dealing with weather and sports), and when you ask if anything is wrong, the caller replies, "Oh, it's nothing," followed by a long awkward silence. What do you say?

7. Break up into pairs again. Think for a moment about someone in your life who could use a word of encouragement over the phone. Make an agreement with your partner to make that call this week.

CHAPTER TEN Helping in the Church

1. The book of Ephesians describes how the church, the body of Christ, can contribute to the people-helping process. Please read Ephesians 4; then make three lists. First, list the characteristics of people helpers in the body (see verses 2-3, 26, 32). Next, list the activities of people helpers in the body (look, for example, at Ephesians 4:12, 15, 22-26, 28-32). Then list the goals of people helpers in the body (see verses

13-14, 28). What does all of this have to do with your activities as a people helper? Please try to be specific.

2. What are the benefits of people helping within the context of the local church? What are the disadvantages?

3. In a group, discuss some of the advantages and disadvantages of helping in a group situation. In what ways have groups made an impact in your life?

4. How well do you think the church is performing its job of being a helping and healing community? What constructive ideas do you have for making the church a more caring place?

5. Break up into groups of four. Discuss what type of people you have a hard time really loving in the church. How can you make changes in this area? Remember to continue to use active listening and empathy when you listen and respond to the other group members as they talk.

6. A couple in your church who has been experiencing financial difficulties has just had a son born with Down's syndrome. How can the church as a whole and individual members provide help and support to this couple?

7. Accepting and loving people, despite their behavior at times, is a cornerstone of effective helping. How accepting are you of people caught in sin and blinded to the truth by Satan? What changes can you make in yourself and in your church to foster a more accepting attitude toward others?

8. Break up into groups of four. Think of some needy people you know. In what tangible ways can you and your church reach out to help these people? Commit to taking action this week!

CHAPTER ELEVEN Helping by Prevention

1. One crucial way to care for others is to do what you can to stop problems before they start. The Bible has many

examples of preventive helping. Discuss the prevention principles found in the following verses: Genesis 2:17; 1 1 ings 19:1-8; Psalms 55:22; 119:9-11; Proverbs 3:5-6; Romans 12:1-2; 2 Timothy 2:15; James 1:19; 1 John 1:9.

2. Break up into pairs, and role-play a preventive helping session. Some topics to consider are: premarital counseling, counseling a young adult headed off to college, or counseling a mother expecting her first child.

3. How is your church involved in preventive helping? What are some suggestions for improvement that you can help to implement in this area?

4. According to the author, what are the ingredients of effective discipleship? Is there anyone in your life whom you could help in these ways?

5. How does the old saying "A stitch in time saves nine" relate to preventive helping? What stitches do you need to start making in the fabric of your life now that will prevent a large tear from appearing later? If you feel comfortable in doing so, share this with someone in your group who could hold you accountable.

CHAPTER TWELVE Helping Yourself

1. The Bible indicates that individuals have a great deal of responsibility for facing and doing something about their own problems. Ephesians 5 gives some guidelines for helping ourselves, and also for preventing future problems. Read Ephesians 5:2-21. What does it mean to walk in love (v. 2; see also vv. 25, 28, KJV), walk in purity (vv. 3-7), walk in the light (vv. 8-14), walk in wisdom (vv. 15-17), and walk in the Spirit (vv. 18-21)? How does this apply to people helping? How does it apply to helping ourselves? Discuss this in your group.

2. Helping ourself starts with an honest assessment of who we are and what areas in our life need growth. Take a few minutes to think about and write down a list of your strengths and weaknesses (spiritual, emotional, intellectual, physical).

3. Break up into groups of four, and share some of the items on your list. Ask for feedback from other group members on what they see as your strengths and weaknesses.

4. The author describes walking in the Spirit as an essential part of helping ourselves and growing in maturity. In very practical terms, what does this walk look like in daily life? What are some of the results of walking in the Spirit?

5. Discovering and developing your spiritual gifts is fulfilling for you and beneficial for others. In looking at the questions the author gives in the chapter concerning discovering your gift(s), what do you think your gift(s) may be? Share this with the group, and ask for their feedback.

6. The self-help movement has become a very big business, especially in North America. What are some of the benefits and some of the dangers associated with this movement?

7. Helpers are often more comfortable helping than receiving help. Are there any areas in your life with which you could use some help right now? Commit yourself to reaching out for that help today. Remember, admitting our weaknesses is a sign of true strength (2 Cor. 12:10).

8. What have you liked best about this book and the study guide? What did you like least? How have you changed as a result of your efforts at becoming a better people helper?